INTO THE PERFORMANCE

INTO THE PERFORMANCE

HEINZ JULEN AND HIS HOTEL IN ZERMATT

INHALTSVERZEICHNIS / CONTENTS

12 / 13 **VORWORT / PREFACE GÖRAN CHRISTENSON**
DIREKTOR KUNSTMUSEUM MALMÖ

90 **INTO THE ARCHITECTURE**
L'ŒUVRE DE HEINZ JULEN DANS LA PERSPECTIVE PATRIMONIALE
MICHEL CLIVAZ

98 **INTO THE ARCHITECTURE**
THE WORK OF HEINZ JULEN FROM THE PERSPECTIVE OF CULTURAL HERITAGE
MICHEL CLIVAZ

106 **IDEOLOGIE UND METHODE**
ANMERKUNGEN ZU DEN WERKEN VON HEINZ JULEN
CHRISTOPH PARADE

112 **IDEOLOGY AND METHOD**
SOME NOTES ON WORKS BY HEINZ JULEN
CHRISTOPH PARADE

130 **EIN HIMMELBLAUER BALKON**
ODER: EINIGE GEDANKEN ZUM WERK VON HEINZ JULEN
CORNELIA PROVIDOLI

134 **A SKY BLUE BALCONY**
OR: A FEW THOUGHTS ON WORK BY HEINZ JULEN
CORNELIA PROVIDOLI

138 **HEINZ JULEN**
INDEX OF WORKS AND BIOGRAPHICAL DATA

«Ich wünsche mir, dass die Menschen diese für sie geschaffene Welt unbelastet und frei erleben – wie ein Kind.»

Heinz Julen

"This world was created for people. They should be carefree in their experience of it – like children."

Heinz Julen

FÖRORD

Heinz Julen, född 1964 i Zermatt, Schweiz, är känd för sitt omfattande konstprojekt *INTO the hotel*. Han hade en vision att bygga ett stort hotell, som han själv skulle designa. Han hade gjort ett tidigare, men då i mindre skala. Heinz Julen köpte en tomt i Zermatt med utsikt över staden och vy mot den berömda bergstoppen Matterhorn. Julen började med att skapa en tunnel till tomten eftersom hotellet skulle ligga på en klippa. Vidare byggdes två hissar för att göra det ännu mer tillgängligt. När Julen höll på med detta insåg han vilken dimension konstprojektet egentligen hade. Hans vän Alex Schärer var lika förtjust över projektet och hade de ekonomiska förutsättningarna. De två vännerna blev partners: Heinz Julen blev ansvarig arkitekturen och designen, Alex Schärer tog hand om den ekonomiska delen. På Heinz födelsedag den 29 februari 2000 öppnade hotellet. Projektet var omskrivet i alla internationella tidskrifter och dagspressen hade noga bevakat hela processen från dess början. Invigningen blev en succé´.

Efter sju veckor stängdes hotellet. Omgivande faktorer utanför hans makt gjorde att det revs.

Hos Heinz Julen finns i sättet att arbeta stora likheter med konstnärerna under renässansen. Han var totalentreprenör. Han utförde byggnadsritningarna, som snarare liknade konstnärliga skisser i sin kraftfullhet och säkerhet. Detta gjorde projektet unikt.

Heinz Julen projekt var också socialt och strukturellt undersökande. Det fanns en ekonomisk sida i projektet som var till gagn för hela orten Zermatt, vilket hade som följd att nästa hela ortsbefolkningen på något sätt var engagerade i projektet.

Normer kan efter ett tag bli stagnerande och förlamande. Heinz Julen vågade och hade förmågan att stå vid sidan av. Han såg att det fanns andra möjligheter som var genomförbara.

Heinz Julen genomförde sin vision – han byggde sitt hotell. Det finns inte längre kvar som objekt. Det som finns kvar är bilderna i denna utställning: Hantverkare, byggnadssnickare, murare samt Alex och hans flickvän. Bildma av Alex och hans flickvän är emellertid inte med på denna utställning, då polisen i Schweiz har beslagtagit dom – på deras begäran. De tyckte det var för stora sexuella anspeglingar i bilderna.

Hans konstprojekt har en konsekvens och tydlighet, som kan sägas vara en fortsättning på de många utställningarna som tidigare visats i F-rummet på Malmö Konstmuseum, där det undersökande och socialt relaterade förhållningssättet är framträdande.

GÖRAN CHRISTENSON
DIRECTOR KUNSTMUSEUM MALMÖ

PREFACE

Up to now, *INTO the hotel* is Heinz Julen's (born 1964 in Zermatt, Switzerland) most comprehensive art project, an exclusive hotel, designed and built by himself. (He had previously built another one, but on a smaller scale.) After he had bought a site overlooking the village Zermatt, with a view of the world-famous Matterhorn, Julen worked on the access to the site. Tunnels had to be blasted as the hotel was meant to be located on a rock. Two elevator-pits were built. While working, the artist became aware of the dimensions of his project. Alex Schärer, a close friend, was equally excited about the idea of building a hotel as an art project. And he had the financial means to make it possible. Thus, the two friends became partners: Heinz Julen was responsible for the concept, the architecture, and the design, Alex Schärer took over the business part.

On Julen's birthday on February 29, 2000, the hotel opened – it was a great success. The project was described in international magazines, and the daily press had already covered the process from the very beginning.

Seven weeks later, the hotel closed. Due to circumstances beyond Julen's control, *INTO the hotel* was torn down.

Heinz Julen's way of working is reminiscent of the artists of the Renaissance. From the tunnelling and the construction down to the very details of choosing the cutlery, he dedicated himself completely to this project. Thus, the hotel in its powerfulness and certainty bore the outlines of an artist. That made it unique.

Of course, this art project also had a commercial side that was beneficial to the village of Zermatt; a lot of people were involved in this project in one way or another. Therefore, *INTO the hotel* can be seen as a social project as well.

Standards can become stagnant and paralyzing. Julen dared to question familiar solutions; he had the stamina to stand up against norms of the Establishment; the result was that he found new ways, new answers.

Heinz Julen realized his vision – he built his hotel. It no longer survives as an object. What remains are the pictures contained in this exhibition: of workmen, carpenters, masons, Schärer and his girlfriend. However, the portraits of Schärer and his girlfriend are not included in the exhibition, as they were confiscated by the Swiss police at their request. They considered them too sexually suggestive.

Julen's art project has a consistency and a clarity that is in continuity with many shows at the F Gallery at Malmö Art Museum, which is devoted to contemporary exhibitions of an investigative and explorative nature.

GÖRAN CHRISTENSON
DIRECTOR KUNSTMUSEUM MALMÖ

INTO yourself

INTO the club

ERST GEGENSÄTZE MACHEN DIE WELT RUND

Das **INTO THE HOTEL** sitzt wie ein Adlerhorst auf einem Felsvorsprung, hoch über Zermatt. Erschlossen wird es direkt von der Bahnhofstrasse über einen Stollen und einen Lift. Durch diesen dringt man ein in den Berg, in eine andere Welt. Dem roh ausgesprengten, indirekt beleuchteten Felsen steht der elegant geschliffene Hochglanzgranit gegenüber.

Zur Rechten: **INTO YOURSELF** – der Meditationsraum. Ein grottenähnlicher, stiller Raum mit dreizehn Video-Monitoren. Jedes Jahr soll ein anderer Künstler, eine andere Künstlerin eine Videoarbeit zum Thema Religion / Spiritualität schaffen. Das Eröffnungsvideo stammt von Heinz Julen; es zeigt den Himmel über Zermatt im Verlaufe eines Tages.

Vis-à-vis: das Gegenstück – **INTO THE CLUB.** Ein lauter Ort, an dem Musik dominiert. Der Club gleicht einer gläsernen Schatulle, beschützt und gleichzeitig bedroht vom Felsen über und unter ihr, rechts und links, hinten und vorne. Bei den Bauarbeiten wurde eine Quelle entdeckt, die nun den unterirdischen See speist, über dem der Club in «unerträglicher Leichtigkeit» zu schweben scheint.

THE WORLD NEEDS CONTRASTS

INTO THE HOTEL perches on a rocky outcrop high above Zermatt like an eagle's nest. It is accessed from Bahnhofstrasse through a tunnel blasted out of the solid rock and by a lift. As visitors penetrate the mountain, they enter a different world. The rough surface of the indirectly-lit rock contrasts with elegant, polished granite.

On the right: **INTO YOURSELF** – the meditation room. A quiet, grotto-like space with thirteen video screens. Each year a different artist will create a religious/spiritual video piece. The first, by Heinz Julen, shows the sky above Zermatt in the course of one day.

Opposite: its counterpart – **INTO THE CLUB.** A resonant place dominated by music. The club is like a glass casket, both protected and threatened by the solid rock surrounding it on all sides. During construction work, a freshwater spring was discovered. This now feeds the underground lake while the club appears to hover over it in "unbearable lightness".

Stollen mit Liftschacht / Tunnel with elevator shaft

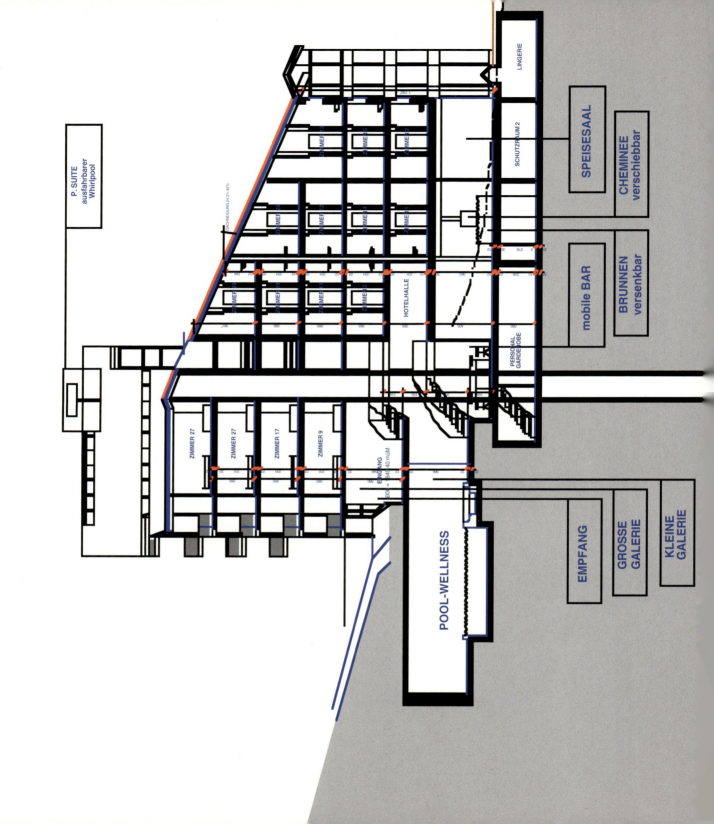

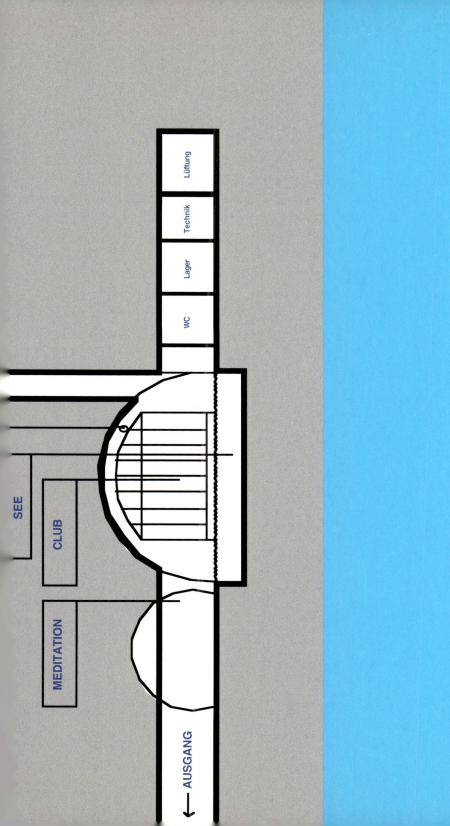

LIEBLINGSSTÜCKE

Heinz Julen arbeitete bereits am *INTO*-Projekt, der Stollen war schon ausgesprengt, die Baupläne bewilligt, als sich sein Freund Alexander Schärer mit seiner Firma USM als Partner anbietet. Die 50:50-Partnerschaft ermöglicht, das Projekt nach den Vorstellungen der beiden Partner zu gestalten – auch finanziell. Präsident der neuen Firma ist Alexander Schärer, Heinz Julen wird Delegierter des Verwaltungsrats. Sein Auftrag lautet, das *INTO* aufzubauen, die *INTO*-Welt zu schaffen. Er ist verantwortlich dafür, dass der Geist des *INTO* beständig durch das Projekt weht; deshalb soll Julen auch nach der Eröffnung als Art Director fungieren.

Anlässlich der Fundamentlegung bringt die Familie Schärer einige Gegenstände mit, die sie einbetonieren will: eine USM-Kugelverbindung (das Herzstück des USM/Haller-Möbelsystems), ein rohes Ei als Fruchtbarkeitssymbol, ein Glas, gefüllt mit internationalen Münzen, als Symbol wirtschaftlichen Erfolgs und eine Ausgabe der USM-Firmenzeitung (von links nach rechts: Tochter Judith, Vater Paul, Mutter Edith, Sohn Alexander Schärer).

Heinz Julen lässt seine Symbolik nicht einbetonieren, sondern hängt sie im Stollen beim Eingang zum Meditationsraum auf: Es handelt sich um eine Jesus-Maria-Assemblage, eines seiner Frühwerke.

Während der Bauphase wird Felsaushub durch den Stollen entsorgt. Ein tonnenschwerer Stein springt aus der Bahn und reisst einen Teil der Fundamentplatte mit sich in die Tiefe – just jenen Teil, in dem die Gegenstände der Familie Schärer einbetoniert sind.

FAVOURITE PIECES

Heinz Julen was already working on his *INTO* project, the tunnel had already been blasted, the building permission had been granted, when his friend, Alexander Schärer, and USM, Alexander's company, offered to join the undertaking as partners. The 50:50 partnership allows the project to proceed according to both partners' intentions – financially as well. Alexander Schärer is the President of the new company, Heinz Julen is on the Board of Directors. He is to build *INTO*, he is to create the *INTO* world and to ensure that the project is imbued with the *INTO* spirit. Therefore, after the opening, Julen is to be appointed *INTO's* Art Director.

On the occasion of the ceremonial laying of the foundation, the Schärer family presentes a few objects to be set into the concrete, namely a USM ball (the key element of the USM/Haller modular furniture system), a raw egg as a symbol of fertility, a jar of coins from all over the world to symbolize economic success, and a copy of the USM company newspaper.

The Schärer family, from left to right: Judith, the daughter; Paul, the father; Edith, the mother; and Alexander, the son.

As he does not wish to have one of his symbols embedded in the concrete, Heinz Julen hangs his in the tunnel, near the entrance to the meditation room. It is one of his early works, a Jesus-and-Mary multiple.

During the construction work, while an excavated rock is taken out through the tunnel, a huge boulder falls from the wagon, pulling part of the foundation plate down with it – precisely the part encapsulating the Schärer family's objects.

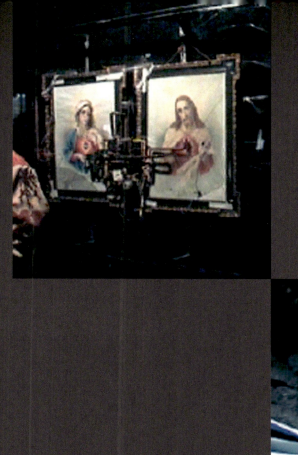

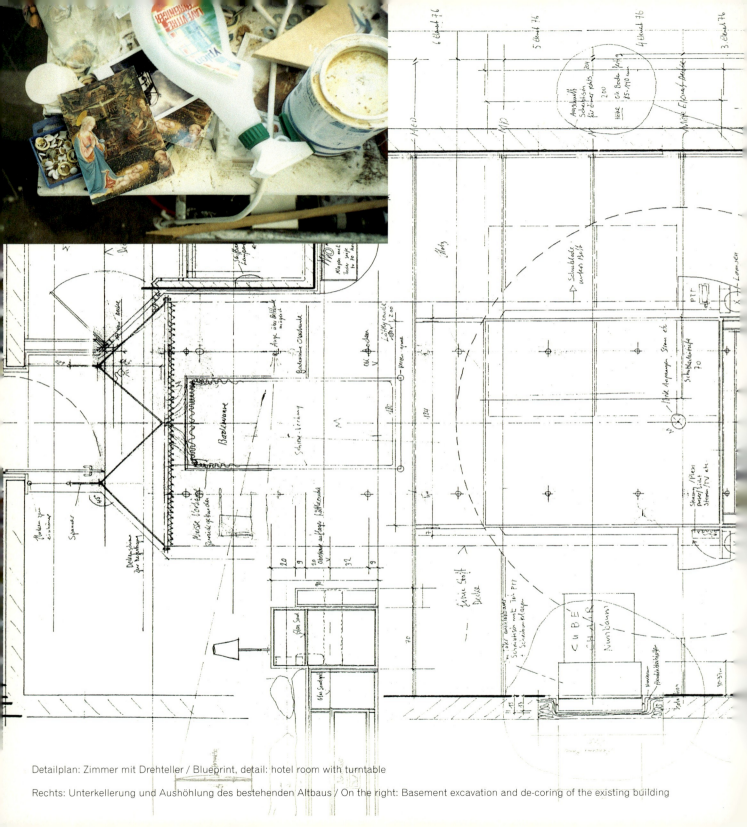

Detailplan: Zimmer mit Drehteller / Blueprint, detail: hotel room with turntable

Rechts: Unterkellerung und Aushöhlung des bestehenden Altbaus / On the right: Basement excavation and de-coring of the existing building

EINE KETTE IST SO STARK...

Heinz Julen realisiert seine Projekte – von der Planung über die Verwirklichung von Bauten bis hin zur Herstellung von Objekten der Inneneinrichtung – in engster Zusammenarbeit mit seinem Team und ausgewiesenen Spezialisten. So entstehen Räume, die in allen Facetten vom gleichen Geist getragen sind. Das Team hat schon zahlreiche Projekte umgesetzt und dabei eine spezifische Arbeitsweise entwickelt: Sehr Vieles wird erst während des Bauprozesses entschieden. Spuren der Handarbeit sind ebenso bewusst gewollt, wie Spuren der Zeit. Die Materialien liegen Julen besonders am Herzen; mehrheitlich stammen sie aus der Gegend. Wenn immer möglich werden sie roh belassen. Befestigungstechniken und Anschlüsse werden oft inszeniert; Funktionalität bestimmt das optische Erscheinungsbild. Julens Bauwerke ähneln in ihrer Entstehung Skulpturen. Seine Mitarbeiter sind aufeinander eingespielt, und über die Jahre hat sich eine gemeinsame Sprache entwickelt. Entsprechend dem jeweiligen Handwerk bilden sich Arbeitsgruppen, im Atelier, auf der Baustelle. Heinz Julen, in ständiger Bewegung, sucht die verschiedenen Gruppen fast stündlich auf, um neue Instruktionen zu geben. Oft wird aufgrund von Skizzen gearbeitet; geht's um einen Prototyp, so legt der Künstler selbst Hand an. So wächst das Projekt gleichsam natürlich und organisch heran. Aufgrund der Grösse und der Komplexität des *INTO*-Projekts sind viele Fremdfirmen beteiligt. Auf Wunsch seines Partners steht Julen zur täglichen Bau- und Finanzkontrolle ein Baufachmann zur Seite. Ohne all diese Menschen ist ein Projekt wie *INTO* nicht denkbar, ohne ihr Engagement, ohne gemeinsame Vision.

A CHAIN IS AS STRONG...

Heinz Julen realizes his projects in closest collaboration with his team and qualified specialists – from the initial project through realizing the buildings to manufacturing fittings and objects for the interiors. All aspects of the spaces created by the team are imbued with the same spirit. The same team has already realized several projects evolving its specific approach. A great many of the key decisions are made during the construction process. Traces of work done by hand are as deliberate as traces of time passing. Julen pays particular attention to the choice of materials, most of which are of local origin and left untreated, whenever possible. Fastenings, anchors, and connections are often emphazised; function determines the visual appearance. Julen's buildings resemble sculptures in the way they are created. The members of his team are perfectly adapted to working with one another, sharing an idiom that has evolved over the years. Depending on the skills required, working groups are formed at the workshop or on the construction site. Always on the move, Julen joins the various groups almost every hour to give new instructions. Work is often based on sketches; if a prototype is required, the artist himself lends a hand. In this way, the project grows almost naturally and organically. The scope and complexity of the *INTO* project requires the involvement of many outside companies. On the partners' request, a building expert helps Julen keep track of daily progress of construction and costs. It is unthinkable to realize a project like *INTO* without all these people, without their commitment and a shared vision.

Eingangshalle mit Lobby und Bar / Entrance hall with lobby and bar

Unterkellerung Altbau;
Aushöhlen und Aussprengen der
zweistöckigen Kunstgalerie

Basement of the existing building;
excavation and blasting of the
two-story art gallery

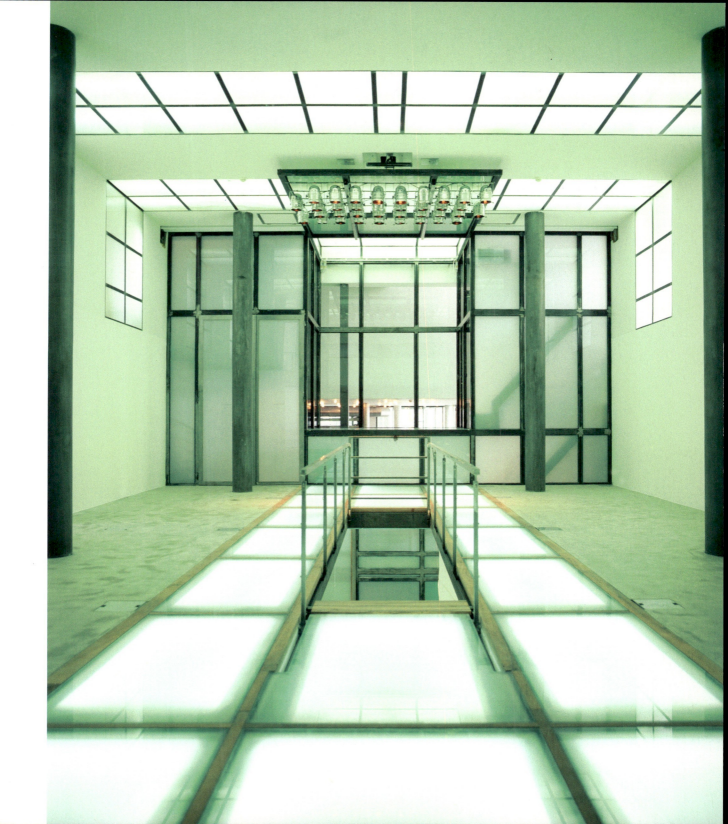

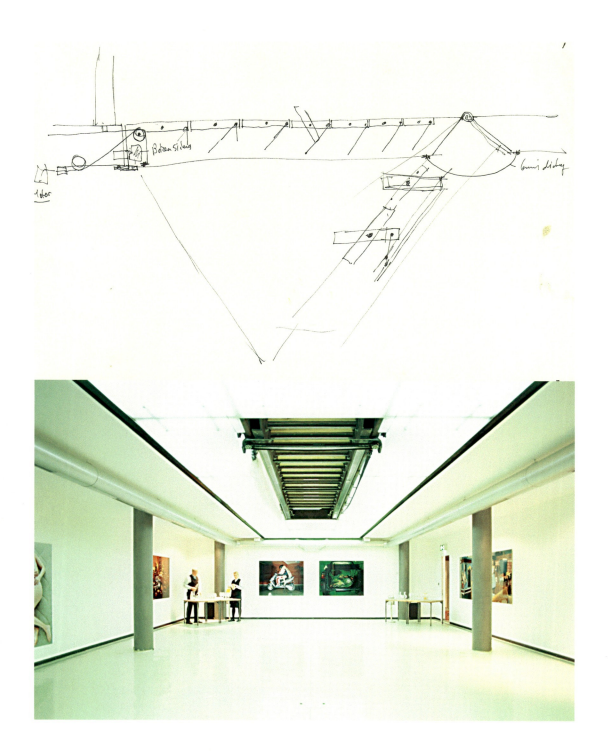

Die Schmetterlingstreppe verbindet die beiden Etagen der Galerie / The butterfly stairs connect the two floors of the art gallery

KUNSTSTÜCKE

Vom Stollen aus gelangen die Gäste per Lift direkt in die Empfangshalle (S. 36–37). Der grosse helle Raum wird von der über dem «Welcome-Desk» sich befindenden gläsernen Bühne dominiert, welche die Empfangshalle von den beiden Ausstellungssälen (S. 40–41) trennt. Wird die Bühne nicht gebraucht, schliesst sie sich mittels einer gläsernen Wand von den Ausstellungssälen ab. Die Wand ist bestückt mit 36 schwenkbaren Bühnenscheinwerfern: Jeder Gast wird hier als Star gesehen, jede hat ihren Auftritt, jeder steht im Rampenlicht.

Das Herz von *INTO* bilden die beiden übereinander liegenden Ausstellungssäle. Zugänglich sind sie von der Lobby aus. Die zentrig angelegte Schmetterlingstreppe verbindet je nach Bedarf die beiden Etagen – eingezogen schafft sie zwei abgeschlossene Räume.

Die Kunst als Fenster, als Pulsfühlerin der weiten Welt prägt das Projekt *INTO*: Anstelle eines Hotelprospektes gibt es jedes Jahr einen neuen Kunstkatalog (entsprechend den stattfindenden Ausstellungen); er vermittelt – jährlich neu – die Philosophie des Hauses: ein Ort der Kunst zu sein. Die Eröffnungsaustellung präsentiert Werke von Olaf Breuning, Balthasar Burkhard, Katrin Freisager, Silvia Gertsch, Chantal Michel, Xerxes Ach.

ARTFUL DEVICES

From the tunnel, the lift carries visitors up to the entrance hall (p. 36–37). The vast, luminous space and the Welcome Desk are dominated by a glass stage above the desk, which separates the entrance hall from the two exhibition galleries beyond (p. 40–41). When the stage is not being used, a glass screen closes off the galleries. 36 adjustable footlights have been set into this screen: each guest is a star, each one is granted his/her great moment in the limelight.

The two exhibition galleries are the heart of *INTO*. They are located one above the other and accessed from the lobby. If required, butterfly stairs placed in the center connect the two levels – when the stairs are closed, the two galleries are separated.

Art is a window onto the world, taking its pulse. Art is at the very core of the *INTO* project. Instead of a hotel booklet, there will be an art catalogue to introduce the exhibitions scheduled to be held each year. This catalogue will promote the philosophy of the house: a "Home to Art". The inaugurating exhibition presents works by Olaf Breuning, Balthasar Burkhard, Katrin Freisager, Silvia Gertsch, Chantal Michel and Xerxes Ach.

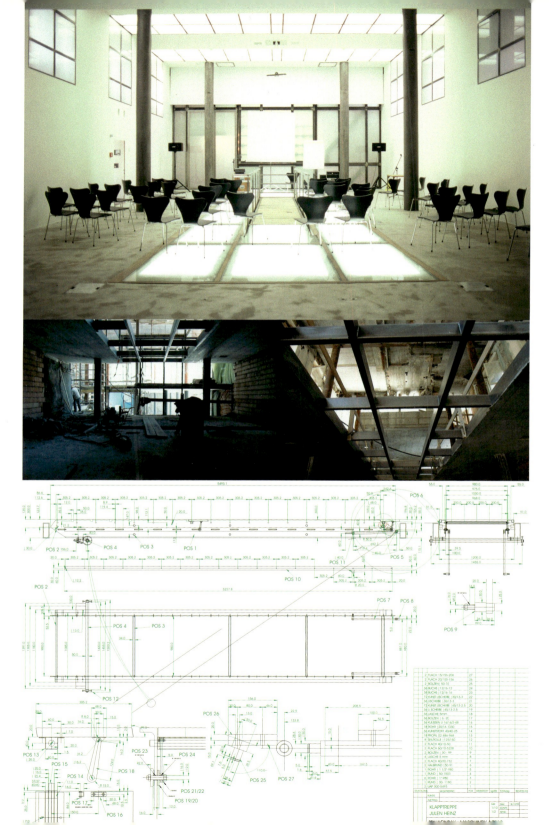

Eröffnung des *INTO the hotel* am 29.02.2000. Die drei Schwestern von Heinz Julen singen ihm ein Geburtstagsständchen: «We are family». Paul und Alexander Schärer überreichen nach der Dankesrede dem an diesem Tag 36-jährigen Künstler ein Geschenk

February 29, 2000: the inauguration of *INTO the hotel*. It was Heinz Julen's 36th birthday. His three sisters serenade him with the song, "We Are Family". Following their thanks, Paul and Alexander Schärer hand Heinz a present

INTO the pool

BLACK & WHITE ODER: VOM DINIEREN UND SINNIEREN

Bei **INTO THE POOL** handelt es sich nicht um ein Schwimmbad. Es ist ein stiller Raum, der zum Nachdenken einlädt. Das Element Wasser wirkt beruhigend und ausgleichend, es trägt und nimmt auf. Das Becken aus Chromstahl, die Wände schwarzer Granit. Vor allem Abends entsteht eine sinnlich-melancholische Stimmung, verstärkt durch die Kerzen, die den Beckenrand säumen. In der Mitte des Raumes schwebt ein riesiger Kronleuchter, bestückt mit Symbolen des Todes. Eine schwermütige Atmosphäre beherrscht das Bad, Wehmut… Es entsteht die Sehnsucht nach Sinnlichkeit, nach Ewigkeit.

Komplementär dazu: der Speisesaal gegenüber. **INTO THE RESTAURANT** inszeniert den Himmel. Beste Kochkünste, edle Weine und hervorragende Bedienung schaffen die Bedingungen für herzliches Zusammensein. In der Mitte des hellen, luftigen Raumes befindet sich die Feuerstelle; sie vermittelt Wärme und Behaglichkeit. Das Feuer flackert 7 cm über der Wasseroberfläche des 3 x 3 m grossen Brunnens, der mittels eines hydraulischen Systems in den Boden versenkt werden kann. Eine Seilkonstruktion dient dazu, die Feuerstelle an einen anderen Ort zu verschieben. Auf diese Weise kann der Charakter des Raumes variiert werden. Riesige weisse Segel an der Decke reflektieren das starke Licht des Brunnens und die Bewegung des Wassers. So entsteht eine elektrisierende, leicht flimmernde Lichtstimmung. Jeder Gast wird beim Betreten des Speisesaals begrüsst: von Engeln, die ihm mit weissen Straussenfedern entgegenwinken. Die Engel befinden sich auf den fünf grossen Kronleuchtern, angetrieben werden sie von Autoscheibenwischer-Motoren.

BLACK & WHITE, OR: ON DINING AND RUMINATING

INTO THE POOL is not a splash or sports pool. It is a quiet space that encourages the bather to engage in introspection. The element of water has a soothing, balancing effect; it is both buoyant and receptive. Especially in the evening, the stainless-steel basin and the black granite walls, as well as the candles placed along the pool's rim create a sensual, melancholy mood. A huge chandelier with symbols of mortality hovers in the center of the room. It is imbued with melancholy and nostalgia … One feels a yearning for sensuality, for eternity.

It is complemented by – **INTO THE RESTAURANT.** Opposite the pool, the dining room symbolizes heaven. Exquisite cuisine, the finest wines and perfect service create a festive mood for cheerful gatherings. Cozy warmth radiates from the fireplace in the center of the spacious, brightly-lit room. The fire crackles seven centimeters above the water in the three-by-three-meter fountain that can be hydraulically sunk into the floor to change the character of the room. A pulley system allows the fireplace to be moved to one side. In this way, the character of the room can be changed. Huge white sails on the ceiling reflect the strong lights and the rippled surface of the fountain. The light shimmering, the atmosphere is discreetly charged. Five enormous chandeliers feature electrically-powered angels waving snow-white ostrich feathers and extending a seraphic welcome to the guests.

Links die verschiebbare Feuerstelle; darunter befindet sich der Brunnen (hier in den Boden versenkt)

On the left, the movable fireplace above the fountain (here shown in the sunken, glass-covered state)

INTO the bar

DIE AUFHEBUNG VON SCHRANKEN

Auf einer runden, im Durchmesser 5 m grossen Metallplatte ist **INTO THE BAR** plaziert. Die Bar ist beweglich, sie kann auf vier Etagen «andocken». Morgens ist sie weit oben, wo die Sonne die Terrasse der Eingangshalle streift, mittags legt sie an bei der Lounge, und abends gesellt sie sich zum Pool, zur Ausstellung oder zum Speisesaal. Je nach Bedürfnis. **INTO THE BAR** ist ein flüchtiger Ort, Blicke werden ausgetauscht, Gespräche entstehen, Schranken werden aufgehoben – auch die Schranken zwischen Dienenden und Bedienten: Um die Bar zu betreten, muss man den Bereich der Dienenden, ihren Arbeitsraum, durchqueren. In der Bar ist ein lockeres, natürliches Zusammensein angesagt; sie funktioniert als Drehscheibe des gesellschaftlichen Lebens im Hotel.

Gletscherähnliche Spalten trennen die vier Häuserblöcke voneinander. Das von oben einfallende Licht bricht sich im Glas und Metall der Treppen und Stege; Blau-, Türkis- und Grüntöne evozieren Bilder von Schnee und Eis. Von hier aus betritt man die Hotelzimmer.

BREAKING BARRIERS

A metal disc five meters in diameter – **INTO THE BAR**. It can dock at four different levels: at the top when the morning sun floods the terrace leading to the entrance hall, or by the lounge on the lower floor at noon. Come evening, it will likely be on the level leading to the exhibition galleries and the dining-room, or down by the pool. It depends on what is needed. **INTO THE BAR** is the place for fleeting encounters, exchanging of glances, striking up conversations, breaking of barriers – even the barrier between those who serve and are served: patrons have to pass through the bartenders' workspace to enter the bar. This is where people come to relax; it is the social pivot of the hotel.

Crevasse-like, deep divides separate the four parts of the building. Light entering from above is refracted by the metal and glass of the stairs and footbridges; blues, turquoises, and greens evoke images of snow and ice. This is the access to the hotel rooms.

INTO the lobby

EIN HOTEL ALS SOZIALE SKULPTUR

Die *INTO*-Eröffnung ist für den 17.12.1999 vorgesehen. So wird denn auch das Hotelpersonal auf Anfang Dezember 1999 eingestellt. Doch die unglücklichen Wetterverhältnisse im Herbst 1999, eine Feuersbrunst im Zimmerbereich sowie vom Wirbelsturm «Lothar» verursachte Schäden am noch nicht ganz fertiggestellten Dach zwingen Heinz Julen und sein Team, die Eröffnung zu verschieben auf das von Alexander Schärer vorgeschlagene Datum, den 29.02.2000. Die Hotelangestellten, bereits vor Ort, entscheiden sich, ob sie Ferientage beziehen oder ob sie auf dem Bau mithelfen wollen. Über 80% des Hotelpersonals zieht Überkleider an und hilft mit, das *INTO* auf den 29.02.2000 hin bezugsfertig zu machen. Elegante Receptionistinnen und trendige Bardamen schleifen Böden, putzen, malen …, derweil die männlichen Hotelangestellten das Hotel einrichten und die Umgebung aufräumen. An der Eröffnungsfeier des *INTO* ist die Stimmung famos, all die Leute, die mitgearbeitet haben, sind stolz auf ihr Werk – und wo gibt es schon ein Hotel, das vom Hotelpersonal fertiggestellt worden ist? Oder fast fertiggestellt … Wie es bei grossen Gebäuden oft vorkommt, ist auch der Bau des *INTO* bei dessen Eröffnung noch nicht vollständig abgeschlossen, so dass die Hotelgäste an dieser Entwicklungsphase teilhaben können.

THE HOTEL AS A SOCIAL SCULPTURE

INTO was to be inaugurated on December 17, 1999. Staff was hired to start at the beginning of the month. However, inclement weather in the autumn of 1999, a fire in the guest-rooms, and damage to the not-quite completed roof, caused by hurricane "Lothar", forces Heinz Julen and his team to postpone the opening. The new date, suggested by Alexander Schärer, is February 29, 2000. The members of staff, who were already here, can decide whether they prefer to take an early holiday or help to complete the hotel. Over 80% of the staff donnes overalls and lends a hand to get *INTO* ready for the guests by February 29. Elegant receptionists and fashion-conscious barmaids sand floors, clean, paint … Their male colleagues install fittings and finish outdoor work. The mood at the inauguration is one of celebration. Everyone involved is proud of their work – where else would you find a hotel that was completed by its own staff? Well, almost completed – as in many large buildings, some work on *INTO* continues after opening-day, allowing the guests to participate in this final stage of its development.

DER WOHLFÜHL-FAKTOR ALS EVOLUTIVES MOMENT

Von den eher kühl wirkenden Korridoren gelangt man in die Hotelzimmer: Oasen der Ruhe, für die Liebe gemacht. Sie sind mit warmem, duftendem Arvenholz ausgekleidet. Der Clou des Zimmers ist die drehbare, im Durchmesser 4 m grosse Metallplatte. Auf ihr sind das Bett, das Sofa und der Tisch angeordnet. Je nach Tageszeit und Bedürfnis ist das Bett mit Blick auf das Dorf, das Matterhorn oder den in die Fensterfront eingelassenen Fernseher gerichtet; tagsüber möchte man vielleicht lieber vom Sofa aus die Aussicht geniessen – also wird auf den Knopf gedrückt, bis die Metallplatte sich in die gewünschte Stellung gedreht hat. Weiter hinten im Raum, anschliessend an die Metallplatte, befindet sich die eigens entwickelte, schwarz eingefärbte beheizbare Betonwanne. Diese steht für das melancholische, meditative Moment und entspricht so dem **INTO THE POOL.** Von der Wanne aus geniesst man den Blick auf das symmetrisch, fast altarbildhaft angelegte Zimmer. Wird die Wanne mit der hölzernen Platte abgedeckt, erinnert sie selbst an einen Altar. Via elektronisch gesteuerten Display kann der Gast verschiedene Stimmungen abrufen: Licht, Wasser, Video, Musik und Duft. Heinz Julen möchte es mit diesen Zimmer-Installationen dem Gast ermöglichen, sich auf sich selbst, seine Wünsche und Sehnsüchte zu konzentrieren, denn nach der Meinung des Künstlers bildet dies eine Bedingung dafür, dass man über sich selbst hinauswachsen kann.

THE COMFORT FACTOR AS AN EVOLUTIONARY DIMENSION

The corridors with their cool atmosphere lead to the hotel rooms: oases of quiet, made for love, lined with the warm, fragrant wood of the Swiss stone pine. The highlight is the turntable, a metal disc four meters across, which accommodates the bed, the sofa, and the table. Depending on the time of day and on the needs of the moment, the bed faces the village, the Matterhorn or the TV set fitted into the window. In the daytime, guests might prefer to enjoy the view from their sofa – at the press of a button, the disc turns into position. Next to the turntable, slightly off centre, stands the custom-designed, heated bathtub in black concrete. It symbolizes the melancholy, meditative dimension of **INTO THE POOL.** Viewed from the tub, the room looks symmetrical, almost reminiscent of an altarpiece. If the wooden lid is in place, the tub itself is altar-like. A computer display allows the guests to adjust the mood of the room, including lighting, water, video, music, and fragrances. Heinz Julen's room installations are intended to help the guests focus on their own wishes and yearnings because, in the artist's opinion, this is one of the key factors that enable people to extend their boundaries.

INTO the room

Handwerker und Hotelangestellte kurz vor der Eröffnung des *INTO* in der Werkstatt

Workers and hotel staff at the workshop, shortly before the inauguration of *INTO*

Die Presidential Suite

The Presidential Suite

Der übers Dach ausfahrbare Whirlpool der Presidential Suite / The Presidential Suite whirlpool; it can be raised above the rooftop

ENTRÜCKUNG UND VERSENKUNG

Per Knopfdruck öffnet sich das Dach, und der sechs Personen fassende Whirlpool wird hydraulisch darüber hinaus ausgefahren: Die Presidential Suite ist zwar nicht nur für Präsidenten gedacht, aber doch für Leute, die sich selbst feiern möchten. Gibt's ein besseres Bild für äusseren Erfolg? Hoch über dem *INTO*, das selbst schon hoch über Zermatt trohnt, zelebriert der Gast im Whirlpool sich selbst und seine Leistungen, er zeigt, dass er etwas erreicht und dieses verdient hat. Doch die Ekstase macht nur Sinn in Zusammenhang mit ihrem Gegenstück, dem Meditationsraum **INTO YOURSELF.** 60 m weiter unten, am tiefsten Punkt des *INTO*, befindet sich dieser Ort der Versenkung, der dieselben Abmessungen aufweist wie der Whirlpool der Presidential Suite.

RAPTURE AND CONTEMPLATION

Press a button, and the roof opens. A hydraulic system slowly raises the whirlpool for up to six people high up into the air. While the Presidential Suite is not intended for presidents only, it is indeed for people looking for a truly special kind of party. Is there a better image for outward success? Floating in this whirlpool perched above *INTO*, which in turn rises high above Zermatt, the guests celebrate their achievements with well-deserved ostentation. However, such ecstasy is meaningful only in the context of its counterpart, the meditation room: **INTO YOURSELF** is situated 60 meters below, at the lowermost point of *INTO*. This place of contemplative immersion has the same dimensions as the Presidential Suite whirlpool.

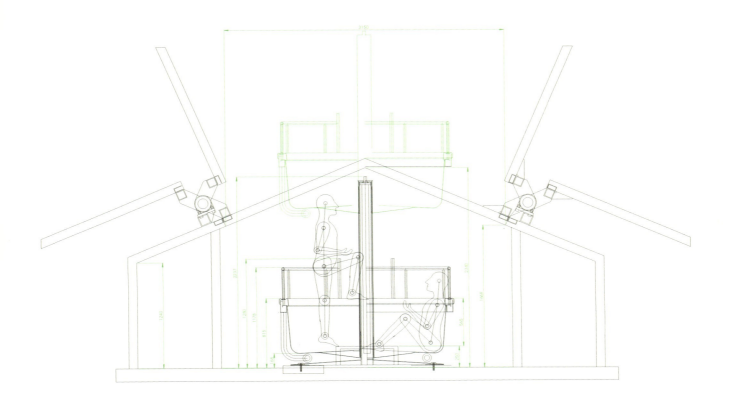

Das *INTO* ist von innen nach aussen gewachsen;
und so reflektiert seine äussere Erscheinung seine
inneren Werte und Funktionen

INTO has grown outwards from inside;
its outer appearance reflects its inner values and functions

DIE RECHTE WANGE ... Das Glück dauert zwei Wochen. Später wird Heinz Julen vom Vater seines Partners und Verwaltungsratspräsidenten Alexander Schärer aus dem Projekt ausgeschlossen. Wo das Geld ist, ist die Macht, halten Edith und Paul Schärer, die Eltern von Alexander, fest. Vom Publikum und den Medien wird Heinz Julen als kreativer Kopf des *INTO* gefeiert. Vielleicht hat das mit dem weiteren Verlauf der Geschichte zu tun. Julen wird verweigert, das *INTO* wie vorgesehen auf den Mai vollständig fertigzustellen, damit das Hotel seinen Betrieb auf die Sommersaison 2000 hin voll umfänglich aufnehmen kann. Sein (ehemaliger) Partner, die Firma USM, engagiert einen eidgenössisch diplomierten Architekten, der dem *INTO* einen «USM-Finish» verpassen soll. Der Architekt hat den Auftrag, das Hotel auf die üblichen konzeptionellen und bauphysikalischen SIA-Normen umzubauen. So wird das gesamte Hotel ausgeräumt und bis auf die rohe Betonkonstruktion entsorgt. Die Familie Schärer will das *INTO* möglichst bald verkaufen.

> Message from Paul to Heinz Julen
>
> The game is over!

THE RIGHT CHEEK... The blissful state lastes two weeks. Later Heinz Julen is expelled from the project by the father of his partner, Alexander Schärer, President of the Board of Directors. Money is power, according to Edith and Paul Schärer, Alexander's parents. The public and the media celebrate Julen as *INTO's* creative mind. This may be relevant to the rest of the story. Julen is not allowed to stay on until May to complete work on *INTO*, so that it could be fully functional in the 2000 summer season. His (former) partner, USM, hires an architect who had graduated from ETHZ, the Swiss Federal Institute of Technology, to graft the "USM finish" onto *INTO*. This architect's brief is to restructure the hotel so that it would correspond to the regular conceptual, static, and physical norms of SIA, the Swiss Association of Engineers and Architects. All the interior fittings are demolished; all that remains is the raw concrete shell. The Schärer family wants to sell *INTO* as soon as possible.

INTO THE ARCHITECTURE
L'ŒUVRE DE HEINZ JULEN DANS LA PERSPECTIVE PATRIMONIALE

MICHEL CLIVAZ

L'histoire de Heinz Julen, que je ne vous conterai pas ici, n'est pas encore recouverte de la précieuse patine historique. Même si son histoire est la sienne et que n'importe quelle histoire n'arrive pas à n'importe qui, son histoire ne lui appartient pas encore totalement contrairement à celle d'Hans Castorp que nous rapporte Thomas Mann dans La Montagne Magique. En effet, Heinz Julen vit, je l'ai rencontré, et son histoire en devenir, partiellement révélée à cet instant présent, appelle un jeu des possibles non encore dévoilé. C'est ce formidable potentiel de talent artistique dont témoigne Heinz que je désire relever. Dans cet espace d'espoir, l'interprétation fera place à l'introspection: *The game is not over but INTO!*

Souvenez-vous d'être venu à Zermatt et que le brouillard vous ait empêché de voir le Cervin? Avez-vous ressenti que malgré ce phénomène, l'ombre de la montagne magique planait des vitrines de la rue de la gare au cimetière, théâtre des événements les plus tragiques qu'elle a toujours engendrés? La présence du célèbre caillou, vous obsédait, même s'il n'était finalement qu'une simple excroissance du continent africain, soulevé par la dérive des continents. Cependant, vos obligations professionnelles devaient vous résoudre à quitter la station, sans l'avoir salué.

Avez-vous remarqué qu'une fois assis confortablement dans le train, votre souvenir de la pyramide emblématique n'était pas du tout affecté par le fait d'avoir ou de ne pas avoir vu l'objet en question? Vous conviendrez, avec étonnement, que l'image mentale que vous reproduisez à ce moment est tout aussi pertinente que celle projetée, par anticipation, avant votre visite ou, par remémoration après votre dernière rencontre. En effet, la reconstruction qui s'opère dans votre esprit comble immédiatement les lacunes de votre observation par des emprunts contractés soit à votre imagination, soit à votre mémoire. L'air de famille de ces multiples reproductions mentales liées à la sensation, à l'imagination ou à l'expérimentation, tant de fois reconnues, parfois reprises, reste à jamais indélébile à travers la vie et la conscience, telle une inscription corporelle de l'esprit. Quelles soient retenues ou partagées, ces images, véritables modèles de la réalité reconstruits à partir de multiples points de vues sur le monde, sont à la base de nos émotions, de nos passions, de notre culture et nous permettent de communiquer.

J'ai eu cette impression, samedi 13 juillet 2002 à 15h35, juste après avoir quitté à la gare de Zermatt, l'enfant sauvage de l'architecture alpine. Nous étions venus, Bénédicte et moi, le rencontrer sur son territoire. Il y avait du brouillard, selon l'expression, à couper au couteau, suisse… Encore une fois, nous n'avions pas pu voir le Cervin. Ce n'est évidemment pas pour la même raison que je nous n'avions pas vu l'*INTO the hotel*. Pourtant, nous avions ressenti étrangement leur présence; leur existence à tous deux était sans aucun doute, pour nous, une certitude. Avaient-ils changé de place pour mieux se cacher? Allaient-ils jeter un cri pour être trouvé à demi? comme dans les poèmes de Rainer Maria Rilke. Allaient-ils venir s'échouer aux portes de la conscience, soulevés par d'étranges dérives, non encore déchiffrées.

Peu importe, maintenant, assis à la fenêtre, suspendus à la crémaillère, la montagne et l'hôtel, se révélaient dans nos esprits par réaction biochimiques et se développaient, de manière photographique, en reproductions mentales multiples. Leur matérialité, soumise à leur observation formelle, n'était, de loin pas, l'unique preuve de leur existence. Si vous avez bel et bien ressenti leur présence, c'est que vous étiez en relation avec une foule d'autres canaux sensoriels qui vous aidaient à prendre conscience des mille et une vies immanentes et transcendantes de chaque objet à travers les multiples manifestations tangibles et intangibles de leur *Genius loci* et de leur *Zeitgeist*.

La valeur spirituelle qui auréole la substance matérielle de tout objet en tout temps et en tout lieu, lui donne sens et autonomie. La rémanence des valeurs immatérielles qualifiant un objet architectural sont-elles plus durables que la corruption des valeurs matérielles et d'usage? Pour le romain encore païen, *etiam ruinae perierunt*, mais pour le chrétien, la révélation porte sur cette survivance de l'esprit après la disparition du corps à travers la résurrection. Il était encore trop tôt pour en avoir le cœur net, mais la passion que Heinz Julen nous dévoilait pour son *Gesamtkunstwerk* révélait les prémisses d'un nouveau monde intérieur patiemment redécouvert et savamment réinventé.

Je pose la mise en perspective du Dessein de l'histoire de Hans en contre-point du Dessin de Heinz. Tous les deux feront légende, à leur manière; car ce n'est pas ni la distance historique ni la tendance prospective qui importent. C'est la nature intime de leurs parcours de vie éminemment symbolique vue à travers quelques signes bien interprétés qui montrent le sens du sacré nécessaire à la recréation d'un mythe. Quelques reliques aident parfois les incrédules; celles rejetées sur le territoire par Heinz diffusent peu à peu, rien ne les arrêtera. Mais les choses ont changé sous leurs apparences universelles. Pour Thomas Mann, l'histoire de Hans Castorp pouvait se raconter en détail, exactement et minutieusement: «*seul est vraiment divertissant ce qui est minutieusement élaboré*» disait-il. Pour un auteur contemporain, l'histoire de Heinz Julen a pour conditions initiales, les exigences de la société du tout numérique. A l'ère du virtuel, la production et la consommation contemporaine de l'imaginaire s'accélère au point d'atteindre la vitesse de libération contre laquelle nous met en garde Paul Virilio. Le temps nous fait cruellement défaut, il nous échappe constamment. Je disposai de sept jours pour cette contribution, il ne m'en reste plus que trois.

Que faire? Fallait-il renoncer à mon engagement? L'histoire de Heinz allait-elle s'achever après les sept semaines mythiques de la première mise en exploitation de l'*INTO the hotel*? Je me remémorais une nouvelle fois les paroles de Heinz sur le nombre symbolique sept. Pensait-il au Dessein de Thomas Mann: «*Ce n'est donc pas en un tournemain que le conteur en finira de l'histoire de Hans. Les sept jours d'une semaine n'y suffiront, non plus que sept mois. Le mieux sera qu'il ne se demande pas d'avance combien de temps s'écoulera sur la terre, tandis qu'elle le tiendra dans ses filets. Après tout, mon Dieu! ce ne seront peut-être pas tout à fait sept années!*»?

Et sur ce, nous commençons.

Tout d'abord l'exemple des boîtes que Heinz Julen avait lancé, quelques années auparavant, depuis la montagne, en direction de la vallée. Après les avoir fait dévaler la pente au cours de cette performance unique, l'artiste les figea derrière une séparation en plexiglas, à la vue des visiteurs d'une exposition étonnante. Pour chaque acte créatif, Heinz Julen aime rejouer la cause initiale, première, quasi divine. Mais les effets sont soumis aux résistances locales. Les aléas de l'événement régissent une histoire, une composition. L'artiste revendique la responsabilité de l'acte créatif comme pour mieux le distinguer de la recréation et de la récréation proprement dite, simple heuristique autorisée au commun des mortels. C'est la métaphore du projeteur qui goûte à l'immense joie de la procréation même si la corruption est déjà programmée.

L'analogie est troublante entre les boîtes blanches de Heinz et les boîtes noires de la pensée humaine. «*On pense comme on se heurte*» disait Paul Valéry[1]. Le penseur doit alors à nouveau, se re-tenir, se re-saisir, se re-dresser, se re-lever, se re-prendre, pour rester debout et se pré-parer à la prochaine re-chute tout en re-pensant déjà à la re-mise en question qui lui succédera. Le travail de Heinz Julen témoigne de cette perte d'équilibre que la pensée engendre, de cette *picnolepsie*[2] et de la re-prise de conscience, qui lui succède aussitôt après, venant compenser cette absence endémique.

Que faire d'autre des boîtes et des concepts cabossés. Deux stratégies opposées mais complémentaires s'offrent alors: la *matrimonialisation* ou la *patrimonialisation*. La première est une pratique, la seconde est une idéologie. La première est une opération naturelle inconsciente, la seconde est une opération culturelle parfaitement consciente. La première conduit les restes aussi bien physiques que psychiques à la décharge pour les recycler, le seconde au musée pour les publier. Marcel Duchamp avait annoncé l'avènement de ce chant(mp) des signes. Heinz Julen proposa aux autorités communales de Zermatt trois lavabos désaffectés hissés sur quatre pieds immergés pour la place devant le *Vernissage*. Les piolets et cordes abandonnés par mégarde ou posés par prudence sur les voies alpines termineront-ils leurs courses à l'ombre ou au soleil? Que dire de sensé à ce propos, dans un monde paradoxal où la décharge est au soleil et à l'air libre alors que le musée est à l'ombre et sous perfusions techniques, l'isolant totalement de son environnement climatique? Le re-jet des restes provient dans la première stratégie de la re-connaissance des défauts et dans la seconde stratégie de la re-connaissance des qualités. Leur re-prise est donc tantôt curative, tantôt épi curative…

La re-prise des restes leurs assignera par conséquent un statut de patrimoine tout en le refusant à ceux qui resteront pour compte. La nouveauté est cependant que ce statut peut alors varier en fonction de la dynamique patrimoniale. C'est également la métaphore du parcours eschatologique du chrétien. A ce jeu, chacun souhaite être reconnu et repris pour la galerie de portraits cabossés exposée au Paradis. Gageons que les œuvres de Heinz sont déjà entrées dans la catégorie des objets d'art et d'architecture élevés au rang de patrimoine!

Mais, c'est une autre histoire, diachronique et lacunaire, que je vous conterai ici, car celle de Heinz, vous l'avez deviné, ce sont nos enfants qui l'écriront et nos petits enfants qui la liront au coin du feu. Les quelques aspects sélectionnés permettront, je l'espère de tisser la toile de fonds nécessaire à une bonne réception du travail de Heinz. Depuis ce degré zéro de l'amour qu'il porte pour toutes ses oeuvres, l'air de la famille *INTO* capture les concepts de boîte, d'hôtel, de salle de cinéma, de loft d'architecture, de soi-même, dans lesquels seront introduit une authentique valeur patrimoniale. Ludwig Wittgenstein s'est beaucoup préoccupé de cet *«air de famille»* qui garantit à chacun de nous la possibilité de reconnaître les siens sans que l'on puisse en détail certifier que ce processus soit unique et identique pour tous les hommes. Ce processus largement inconscient conduit à la reconnaissance et à la valorisation du patrimoine par un individu ou une collectivité culturelle quelconque et à sa reprise.

Quel est le degré de parenté des œuvres de Heinz Julen? Par une étrange ressemblance, les quatre cas de nature différente que je me propose d'évoquer, partagent en commun, de manière universelle et durable, les valeurs matérielles et immatérielles attribuées à toute famille patrimoniale. Ces objets peuvent ainsi appartenir à un ensemble patrimonial pour autant que cette qualité demeure fixée à son substrat physique ou psychique indépendamment des circonstances et du contexte référentiel. Ils nous apporteront les conditions nécessaires à la constitution d'une famille patrimoniale et les limites suffisantes à la reconnaissance patrimoniale et à la reprise de ses composants. Chacun de ces cas nous apportera sa propre contribution à la définition du processus complexe de patrimonialisation: de l'héritage, nous passerons à la revendication et à la ré-appropriation et nous rencontrerons, finalement, la re-composition.

1. PATRIMOINE HERITE: LE VERNISSAGE ET LE CONCEPT DE L'ARCHITECTURE ALPINE

Pour l'architecte moderne et contemporain, construire en milieu alpin a toujours été un stimulant favorable à la recherche et au développement de solutions techniques, fonctionnelles et plastiques. C'est dans ce sens que s'exprimait Bruno Reichlin dans son article *«Quand les architectes modernes construisent en montagne»* dans lequel il notait que: «*l'architecture de montagne ou alpine, des modernes ou des contemporains peu importe, est surtout une hypothèse de travail pour la critique architecturale et une stimulation culturelle pour le projet*». Le territoire alpin conjugué avec les intentions et les anticipations des projeteurs a donc été pour le développement de l'architecture du XXème siècle un creuset expérimental fertile. Qu'en est-il aujourd'hui? Si les Alpes représentent, depuis les années 20, un formidable terrain d'aventure pour les modernes, c'est également sur cette besogneuse terre d'expérimentation que la tradition s'y perpétue, mieux qu'ailleurs: terre paradoxale d'accueil et de répulsion, de conservation et d'innovation.

Heinz avait ressenti depuis son plus jeune âge, le potentiel d'expérimentation qu'il pouvait tirer de son atelier dans les montagnes, tantôt tente éphémère, tantôt refuge d'altitude. Avec pour tout bagage, ses premières expériences d'habitat éphémère et ses formidables dons pour l'artisanat du bois et de la construction métallique, l'enfant sauvage de l'architecture alpine collecte les vieilles boiseries, les madriers démontés, les tableaux de la vierge et des saints, les pièces usagées des installations de remontées mécaniques, pour mieux les remettre en scène au *Vernissage*. Plus il invente, plus il récupère, moins il dessine à l'atelier, plus il compose sur le chantier… Ses investigations sont des reconnaissances, ses œuvres sont des reprises! Dans sa forge accrochée à la montagne, plus Heinz perpétue les savoir-faire, plus il intensifie son savoir être…

Le concept d'architecture alpine ne tient plus pour les *Bains de Vals* de Peter Zumthor, pas plus que pour le *Vernissage* d'Heinz Julen. Nul besoin d'un concept construit à posteriori. C'est à l'intérieur que le projet s'agite. Les étages inférieurs du bâtiment familial sont placés sous le signe des découvertes et des rémanences. Le chantier est le théâtre d'un projet sans cesse redécouvert et réinventé. Le monde clos, autonome du cinéma requiert pour sa mise en scène un art total, une véritable machine à projeter, à voyager. Une atmosphère chaleureuse émerge à travers une matérialisation cahoteuse. Une liberté formelle se dégage de l'intérieur mûrement réfléchit, constamment enrichit…

Avec le *Vernissage*, nous apprendrons que le patrimoine peut être hérité; il porte les germes féconds d'un mouvement, d'une tendance, de la constitution de sa propre famille patrimoniale…

2. PATRIMOINE REVENDIQUE: LE VIEW HOUSE ET L'ANTHROPOLOGIE DU PROJET

La vie procède, depuis son apparition, par processus d'anticipation, c'est-à-dire, par projet. De même pour l'homme. Comment Michel-Ange trouvait-il dans son bloc de marbre de Carrare le personnage qu'il avait conçu au préalable dans son imagination? A la Renaissance, l'homme avait déjà la maîtrise de la taille et de la sculpture de la matière. Mais comment tailler et sculpter de manière consciente la matière et l'esprit à l'ère de la société des télécommunications et des internautes?

Heinz Julen s'active à l'intérieur du bloc de marbre. C'est de l'intérieur qu'il compose. Il se déplace dans un autre lieu, le lieu du projet intérieur avec ses propres méthodes d'anticipation bien particulières, tout en demeurant présent au monde. L'ubiquité qu'il pratique est le don le plus étrange qu'il possède, pur esprit en même temps qu'artisan. Intellectuel aussi bien que manuel, il en use pour ses enquêtes et ses recherches sur le terrain comme au plus profond de lui-même. Heinz joue aussi bien le rôle du touriste, de l'entrepreneur, du régisseur qu'il connaît à fond; tout est fait pour le plaisir des sens, la célébration du couple, le culte des valeurs ludiques… Le paysage pénètre dans la chambre, la télévision se projette à l'extérieur, le lit jouxte la baignoire sans aucune difficulté, parfois même il tourne. Son travail de chasseur – cueilleur laisse place à celui de concepteur – constructeur.

Avec le *View House*, nous apprendrons que le patrimoine peut être revendiqué; il porte les signes distinctifs d'un langage, d'une échelle de valeurs, d'un air de famille labellisé…

3. PATRIMOINE RE-APPROPRIE: L'INTO THE HOTEL ET LA NOUVELLE ALLEGORIE DU PATRIMOINE

La mutation qu'a subit la notion de patrimoine ces dernières années fait que ce ne sont plus seulement les grands monuments marqués par l'histoire qui sont l'objet d'une protection et d'une conservation, mais toutes sortes d'édifices. Au côté des constructions vernaculaires, des équipements touristiques ou des infrastructures paysagères, les hôtels entrent dans la catégorie des objets construits élevés au rang de patrimoine. Une véritable petite révolution copernicienne a affecté le paradigme patrimonial. A travers le patrimoine de type social et communautaire se déchiffre une identité de groupe. L'enracinement local soutient le développement régional. De matériel et visible, le patrimoine est devenu invisible et symbolique. Il évolue d'un sens matériel et privé à un sens immatériel, public et métaphorique pour finalement échapper à son propre auteur à travers les enjeux posés par les acteurs sociaux. De restreinte, la patrimonialisation devient générale. Cette nouvelle allégorie du patrimoine contribue à la reconsidération de l'ensemble de la production du cadre bâti du XXème siècle.

C'est alors que l'éclair de la compréhension me traversa une nouvelle fois l'esprit. La révélation que me faisait Heinz avec son hôtel était douloureuse, car un vent de révolte était passé par là. Rodin nous avait pourtant clairement averti, que, *trop pure, la cathédrale provoque un vent de dédain.* Je m'explique: sept semaines, c'est juste le temps nécessaire pour que l'œuvre que Heinz aimait tant prenne corps et que soufflent le génie du lieu et l'esprit du temps. A travers cette matérialisation éphémère, une âme était née. Tant qu'il y aura des hommes, l'esprit de l'*INTO* devenait immortel et plus rien ne pouvait le détruire.

Tard-venu de la création,
oeuvre du huitième jour, posthume.
Puisque c'est nous qui te faisons,
il faut croire que Dieu te consume.

Avec l'*INTO the hotel*, nous apprendrons que le patrimoine peut être ré-approprié; il possède tous les ingrédients de l'appartenance au sacrifice patrimonial et à son itération qu'il postule au sens de Jean-Pierre Babelon et André Chastel[3]: *«Peut-être faut-il rappeler que dans toute société le patrimoine se reconnaît au fait que sa perte constitue un sacrifice et que sa conservation suppose des sacrifices?»*

4. PATRIMOINE RE-COMPOSE: LE LOFT ET LA PROSPECTIVE OUVERTE

Avec le *Loft*, Heinz Julen retrouve l'esprit de l'atelier de montagne, de sa cabane d'enfant, de l'éphémère, du potentiel encore inexploité, de l'œuvre ouverte chère à Umberto Eco, partiellement réalisée, globalement interprétée.... L'ascenseur inachevé, la baignoire récupérée, le mobilier remis en scène, tout participe du même air de famille comme le sensuel rideau blanc qui vient caresser le Bon air des Alpes. Dans le contexte contemporain de métamorphose permanente, la question n'est plus seulement d'observer le monde et de reconstruire son double à la perfection, mais bel et bien d'ouvrir de nouvelles perspectives à partir de points de vues multiples et de recréer des mondes possibles, surdéterminés. La carte ne représente plus le territoire mais se distingue totalement de celui-ci et de sa relation incestueuse en s'attribuant sa propre autonomie et en lui assignant des dimensions insouçonnées, comme pour les œuvres de Mannette Fusenig exposées au *Vernissage*.

Avec le *Loft*, nous apprendrons que le patrimoine peut être re-composé; une chambre de l'hôtel est remontée avec sa façade et ses équipements sanitaires, voire son mobilier; le projet devient projet de re-connaissance et projet de re-prise, son processus est un processus anthropologique de recréation. L'héritage et la revendication patrimoniale s'allient alors à la stratégie de la ré-appropriation et soutiennent la recomposition du patrimoine à partir de ses restes ...

Comme on pouvait s'y attendre, l'histoire de Heinz Julen n'est pas nouvelle. Lorsque Hiram eut fini son œuvre, David la trouva si belle qu'il pensa qu'elle lui porterait ombrage. Craignant pour son pouvoir et son autorité, le roi se priva des services du maître maçon et il le renvoya sur les sables phéniciens sans pouvoir lui soustraire son formidable secret. Malgré des destructions successives, l'œuvre survécut pourtant aux morsures du temps car sa charge émotionnelle a très rapidement surpassé sa présence matérielle. Aujourd'hui, la mémoire du temple de Jérusalem gravée dans les pierres du mur des lamentations témoigne encore des innombrables conflits entre communautés religieuses belliqueuses. Pour le meilleur et pour le pire, durant le XXème siècle, les plus grandes pensées ont ainsi côtoyés les plus grandes bêtises en matière de patrimoine: les Halles de Paris, disparues,....on pourrait reprendre la rengaine de Serge Gainsbourg sur les disparus des 60'. Le vandalisme est encore présent sous nos yeux. Pour célébrer le sacrifice patrimonial, il n'était donc pas nécessaire d'aller chercher des références jusque sur la route de la soie. Chacun sait que le mensonge engendre la destruction. *Mensonge, jouet que l'on casse* disait Rainer Maria Rilke.

Heinz Julen souffre. Prométhée avait payé un lourd tribu aux dieux pour avoir trop approché la connaissance. La tradition judéo-chrétienne avait inventé l'année du Jubilée pour effacer les dettes et accorder le pardon. L'année du grand Jubilée de l'an 2000 en fut un témoignage retentissant. Dans les glaciers et les parois rocheuses du Cervin, l'écho du chant traditionnel alpin, le Yodel, en est un rappel émouvant. A Zermatt comme à Münsingen, il faut savoir que Jubilée et Yodel ont la même origine étymologique. La musique du *Loft* appelle le pardon.

Maintenant que le paysage défile lentement sous nos yeux je me remémore, après tant d'émotions, les phrases de l'auteur des Quatrains valaisans:

Sanglot, sanglot, pur sanglot!
Fenêtre, où nul ne s'appuie!
Inconsolable enclos,
plein de ma pluie!

C'est le trop tard, le trop tôt
qui de tes formes décident:
tu les habilles, rideau,
robe du vide!

Si Heinz Julen, le moniteur de ski, devait nous révéler un secret, se serait celui de l'amour qu'il porte pour sa famille patrimoniale. A ce jeu-là, il n'y a que des gagnants: le client, le concepteur, l'utilisateur, l'artisan, le personnel de maison, l'architecture…

Le rideau se lève et retombe chaque soir au *Vernissage*, au *View House*, au *Loft;* la chorégraphie ne fait que commencer, j'aperçois déjà ta prochaine œuvre, Heinz, jamais la même, mais toujours reconnaissable; elle a déjà un petit air de famille…

A ton futur projet, Heinz!

---

1 VALERY Paul, Cahiers, Tomes 1&2, Encyclopédie de la Pléiade, Gallimard, Paris, 1973, 1974
2 au sens que lui donne Paul VIRILIO dans son *Esthétique de la disparition*
3 BABELON Jean-Pierre et CHASTEL André, *La notion de patrimoine*, in *Revue de l'Art*, n°49, 1980, Liana Levi, 1995

INTO THE ARCHITECTURE
THE WORK OF HEINZ JULEN FROM THE PERSPECTIVE OF CULTURAL HERITAGE[1]

MICHEL CLIVAZ

Heinz Julen's story, which I will not tell you here, has not yet acquired a historical patina. Even if a story doesn't happen to just anyone, his story is not yet entirely his own, unlike Hans Castorp's in Thomas Mann's *Magic Mountain*. Indeed, Heinz Julen lives. I have met him, and have followed his story in the making, part of which is being revealed right now, evoking not-yet-unveiled potentialities. It is his great artistic talent that I wish to address here. In this space of hope, interpretation will give way to introspection: *INTO – the game is not over!*

Did you ever come to Zermatt when the fog prevented you from seeing the Matterhorn? Did you perhaps feel the spectre of this magic mountain hovering over the shop windows of the street that leads from the train station to the cemetery, the scene of tragic events? Were you perhaps entranced by the presence of the famous "rock", even though it was, after all, but a simple outgrowth of the African continent, brought here by continental drift? Still, you would have allowed your professional duties to prevail, leaving without having saluted the peak.

Did you notice that, once you were comfortably installed on the train, your memory of the emblematic pyramid wasn't at all affected by the fact that you might or might not have seen the actual object? You will agree that the memory of it right now is as pertinent as the one projected in anticipation, before your visit, or at any time since. Indeed, the reconstruction that occurs in your mind immediately fills the gaps in your observation by borrowing either from your imagination or your memory. The family likeness of these multiple mental reproductions linked to feelings, imagination, or experimentation – so often recognised, sometimes recovered – remains indelible forever throughout life and consciousness, like a physical inscription of the mind. These images are models of reality, reconstructed from multiple points of view of the world. They are the foundation of our emotions, passions and culture; they allow us to communicate with each other.

This is how I felt on the afternoon of July 13, 2002, having left the wild child of alpine architecture at Zermatt train station. We had come, Benedict and I, to meet him on his territory. It was so foggy, it felt as though one could have cut it with a Swiss army knife ... Once again, we could not see the Matterhorn. Likewise, we could not see *INTO the hotel,* albeit for a different reason. Strangely, though, we clearly felt their presence; without a doubt they both existed. Had they moved elsewhere to hide? Would they cry out to be half-found, as in one of Rainer-Maria Rilke's poems? Would they be deposited at the doors of our conscience, brought there by a strange, as yet undeciphered fate?

Little does it matter now, as we're sitting at the window of the cog-wheel train descending the steep track. The mountain and the hotel revealed themselves in our minds through biochemical reactions and were developing, photograph-like, into multiple mental reproductions. To actually see them was by far not the only proof of their existence. They made their presence felt because we were in tune with a slew of other sensory impulses that enabled us to become aware of the immanent and transcendental one thousand and one lives of each object through countless revelations of their *Genius loci* and their *Zeitgeist*.

The spiritual value that envelops the material substance of each object imbues it with meaning and autonomy. Does the after-image of the immaterial values of an architectural object outlast the corruption of its usefulness and material value? For the Roman who is still a pagan, *etiam ruinae perierunt*. For the Christian, however, the key to revelation is the survival through resurrection of the spirit after the body has disappeared. It was still early days for any certainty, but the passion for his *Gesamtkunstwerk* that Heinz Julen allowed us to glimpse revealed a patiently rediscovered and wisely reinvented inner world.

I have contrasted Hans Castorp's story with Heinz Julen's. Both will be legends, in their own right. The intimate nature of their eminently symbolic life journeys, seen through a few well-interpreted signs, shows the meaning of the sacred that is needed to recreate a myth. A few relics sometimes help those who do not believe; nothing is to stop those dispersed by Julen from taking hold. However, beneath their universal appearance things have changed. For Thomas Mann, Castorp's story could be told in meticulous detail: "Only that which is minutely detailed is truly entertaining." To a contemporary author, Julen's story contains all the trappings of digital society. In a virtual age, the production and consumption of make-believe accelerates so rapidly that it reaches the speed of liberation of which Paul Virilio has been warning us. We desperately lack time; we are constantly running out of time. I had seven days to write this contribution; now there are only three.

What was there to be done? Should I abandon my contribution? Would Julen's story end after the seven mythical initial weeks that *INTO the hotel* was operational? I again recalled his words concerning the symbolic number seven. Was he remembering Thomas Mann? *It is not in a trice that the narrator will accomplish Hans's story. The seven days of a week will not suffice, nor will seven months. The best thing will be for him not to wonder, whilst he finds himself held in its nets, how long he will be on earth. After all, my God! it may not take quite seven years!*

On this note, let us commence.

Let us consider the example of the cubes that, some years ago, Heinz Julen tossed from a mountain. Once they had tumbled down the slope in this unique performance, the artist placed them behind a plexiglass divider in plain sight of the visitors of an amazing exhibition. In each of his own creative acts, he likes to replay the original, quasi-divine cause. Its effects, however, are subjected to local resistance, and their history, their composition is governed by the aleatory. The artist claims responsibility for the creative act so as to better distinguish it from re-creation and the kind of recreation ordinary mortals may enjoy. Like the metaphorical architectural designer, he tastes the great joy of procreation even though corruption has already set in.

The analogy between Julen's white boxes and the black boxes of human thought is disturbing. "We think as we hurt ourselves," Paul Valéry[1] once said. The thinker must thus re-tain and re-turn himself to his former position, so as to re-main standing and pre-pare himself for the next re-lapse, all the while re-thinking the re-consideration that will ensue. Julen's work shows this loss of balance that is engendered by thought, this picnolepsy[3] and the re-covered awareness, which follows immediately and which compensates for this endemic absence.

What else can be done with battered boxes and concepts? Two contrasting yet complementary strategies offer themselves: *matrimonialisation* or *patrimonialisation*. The first is a practice, the second an ideology. The first is an unconscious natural operation; the second is a perfectly conscious cultural operation. The first leads the remainders, both physical as well as psychological, to the dump for recycling, the second to a museum for display. Marcel Duchamp announced the advent of this song and field[4] of signs. Heinz Julen's gift to Zermatt was three disused washbasins on four legs, installed on the square in front of *Vernissage*. What is the meaning of this, in a paradoxical world where the dump is exposed to the sun and open air, whereas the museum is in the shade and on technical IV, in complete isolation from its environment? In the first strategy, the re-jection of the remainders is due to the re-cognition of defects and, in the second, the re-cognition of qualities. Their re-using is thus at times curative, at times epi-curative …

Remainders that are being re-used will therefore obtain patrimony status. What is new, however, is that patrimonial dynamics may alter this status. This is also a metaphor for a Christian's eschatological path. In this game, everyone wants to be recognized and taken to the battered portrait gallery exhibited in Heaven. The wager is on that Julen's works have already achieved patrimony status!

However, there is another diachronic and fragmentary story that I am about to tell. May a few selected aspects allow to create a backdrop for due appreciation of Julen's work. In the primordial passion that he has for all of his works, the *INTO* family likeness captures the concepts of night-club, hotel, cinema, architectural studio, *Loft*, of self, which will be imbued with an authentic patrimonial value. Ludwig Wittgenstein has thought deeply about this "family likeness", which grants to each one of us the gift of recognizing our own without being able to claim that this process is unique and identical for everyone. This largely unconscious process leads to a recognition and re-valuing, and to a revival, of patrimony.

What degree of kinship is there in Heinz Julen's works? By a strange resemblance, the four different cases that I propose to address share the material and immaterial values attributed to all patrimonial families. Each of these cases will make its own contribution to the definition of the complex process of patrimonialisation, from heritage, through claiming and re-appropriation, to re-composition.

1. INHERITED PATRIMONY: VERNISSAGE AND THE CONCEPT OF ALPINE ARCHITECTURE
For the modern contemporary architect, building in the alpine environment has always been a stimulus to research and develop new technical, functional and architectural solutions. It is in this sense that Bruno Reichlin noted in his article, "When Modern Architects Build in the Mountains": *mountain or alpine architecture, be it modern or contemporary, is above all a working hypothesis for architectural criticism and a cultural stimulation for the project.* For architectural designers, the alpine territory was thus a fertile ground for experiments in 20th century architecture. Where does it stand today? If, since the 1920s, the Alps have been an extraordinary playing-field for modern architects, it is on this same territory that tradition has been perpetuated, more than elsewhere – a paradoxical situation.

Even when he was little, Julen felt the potential for experimentation that he could get out of his mountain workshop, which at times was an ephemeral tent, at times a high-altitude refuge. Equipped only with his early experiences in ephemeral habitats and his extraordinary gift for woodworking and metal construction, the wild child of alpine architecture collected old panelling, discarded beams, battered paintings of the Virgin and saints, used spare parts from ski lifts, etc., which he proceeded to present at *Vernissage*. The more he invents, the more he recovers, the less he draws in his workshop, the more he sketches his designs on the construction site … His works are revivals! In his forge perched high up in the mountains, the more skills he acquires, the greater his savoir vivre …

The concept of alpine architecture no longer holds for *Bains de Vals* by Peter Zumthor, nor for *Vernissage* by Heinz Julen. No need for a concept built à *posteriori*. It is from within that the project comes to life. The lower stories of the family building hold discoveries and memories. The construction site is the stage for a project that is constantly being rediscovered and reinvented. For its performances, the closed, independent world of the cinema requires total art, a veritable projector, a travelling machine. A warm atmosphere emerges from rough materialisation. A formal liberty is released from within, after much thought which has made it richer …

Vernissage teaches us that patrimony can be inherited; it bears the fertile seeds of a movement, a trend, the constitution of one's own patrimonial family …

2. CLAIMED PATRIMONY: VIEW HOUSE AND THE ANTHROPOLOGY OF A PROJECT

Since its earliest beginnings, life has been propelled by the process of anticipation, by projects. The same is true for man. How did Michelangelo find in his block of Carrara marble the figure that he first conceived in his mind? By the time of the Renaissance, man had already mastered the art of carving and sculpting materials. But how does one consciously sculpt and carve mind and matter in our telecommunication and Internet society?

Heinz Julen composes from within the marble block. He moves in a different space, that of the inner project with its own ways of anticipating, all the while remaining present in our world. The ubiquity that he practices is the strangest gift, pure spirit as well as artisan. Both intellectual and manual, he uses this gift in his surveys and research, both in the field and deep within himself. Julen perfectly plays all the roles, that of the tourist, the entrepreneur, the director; everything is done for the pleasure of the senses, the celebration of the couple, the worship of ludic values. The outside penetrates into the bedroom, the TV set is projected outside, the bed is in effortless juxtaposition with the bathtub – sometimes it even turns. His work as a hunter-gatherer gives way to that of designer-constructor.

View House teaches us that patrimony can be claimed; it bears the distinct signs of an idiom, of a set of values, the stamp of a family likeness ...

3. RE-APPROPRIATED PATRIMONY: INTO THE HOTEL AND THE NEW ALLEGORY OF PATRIMONY

The change which the notion of patrimony has undergone in the last few years is such that not only the great monuments that have been marked by history are the object of protection and conservation, but rather all types of structures. Next to vernacular construction, tourist facilities, or landscaped infrastructures, hotels are being included in the category of built objects that have attained the status of patrimony. A small Copernican revolution has affected the patrimonial paradigm. Group identity has come to depend on social and community-type patrimony. Local roots support regional development. From being material and visible, patrimony has become invisible and symbolic. From having a material and private meaning it has acquired an immaterial, public and metaphorical meaning and has, at last, escaped its own author in the stakes claimed by social actors. From being restrictive, patrimonialisation has become general. This new allegory of patrimony contributes to a reconsideration of the entire architectural production of the 20th century.

It was at this point in my musings when comprehension once again flashed through my mind. Julen's hotel had offered me a painful revelation, for the wind of revolt had stormed through it. Rodin clearly warned us that, *too pure, the cathedral stirs the wind of disdain.* Let me explain: seven weeks, this is exactly the time needed for the work that Julen loved so much to take form, and for the genius of the place and the spirit of time to breathe. This ephemeral materialisation gave birth to a soul. For as long as there are people, the spirit of *INTO* will be immortal; it is indestructible.

Latecomer of creation,
Work of the eighth day, posthumous.
Since it is we who make you,
One must believe it is God who consumes you.

INTO the hotel teaches us that patrimony can be re-appropriated; it possesses all the ingredients required of patrimonial sacrifice alluded to in the words of Jean-Pierre Babelon and André Chastel[5]: *Maybe it should be recalled that in any society, patrimony is recognized by the fact that its loss constitutes a sacrifice and that its conservation implies sacrifices.*

4. RE-COMPOSED PATRIMONY: LOFT AND THE OPEN PROSPECT

Loft helps Heinz Julen rediscover the spirit of the mountain workshop, of his childhood cabin, of the ephemeral, not-yet-achieved potential, of the open work dear to Umberto Eco, partially completed, globally interpreted… The unfinished lift, the salvaged bathtub, the furniture returned to its proper place – everything is part of the same family likeness as the sensual white curtain that is caressed by the beneficial mountain air. In the contemporary context of perpetual metamorphosis, the issue is not only to observe the world and to rebuild its perfect replica, but rather to open up new perspectives from multiple viewpoints and to recreate possible, perhaps overdetermined worlds. The map no longer represents a territory; it is a completely different thing, which has abandoned its incestuous relationship by appropriating its own autonomy and undreamt-of dimensions, as in the works by Mannette Fusenig shown at *Vernissage*.

Loft teaches us that patrimony can be re-composed; one of the rooms of *INTO the hotel* has been reconstructed, down to the façade, plumbing and furniture; in an anthropological process of recreation, the project has become one of re-cognition and re-use. Heritage and patrimonial claims thus unite with the strategy of re-appropriation and support the recomposition of patrimony from its remainders …

As might have been expected, Heinz Julen's story is not new. When Hiram had finished his work, David thought it was so beautiful that he feared it might overshadow him. Fearing for his own power and authority, the king deprived himself of the services of his master builder, returning him to the Phoenician sands without having been able to discover his powerful secret. Despite subsequent destruction, the masterpiece has stood the test of time, for its spiritual value very soon exceeded its material presence. The memory of the temple of Jerusalem engraved in the stones of the Wailing Wall still bears witness to the strife between bellicose religious communities. With regard to patrimony, for better or for worse, during the 20th century, the greatest ideas thus rubbed shoulders with the most abject stupidity: *les Halles de Paris, disparues,…* we could add to Serge Gainsbourg's old song on what was destroyed in the 1960s. Vandalism still insults our eyes. To celebrate patrimonial sacrifice, there is no need to look as far back as the Silk Road. Everyone knows that lies engender destruction. Lies are the toys we break, as Rainer-Maria Rilke has said.

Heinz Julen has suffered. Prometheus had to pay a heavy tribute to the gods for having come too close to knowledge. The Judeo-Christian tradition invented the year of the Jubilee to erase debts and give pardon and Jubilee 2000 bore resounding witness. Among the glaciers and the rock faces of the Matterhorn, the echo of the traditional alpine song, the Yodel, is a moving reminder. In Zermatt as in Münsingen, it should be noted that the words Jubilee and Yodel have the same etymological origin. The music of Loft calls for pardon.

Now that the landscape slowly passes in front of our eyes, after so many emotions I recall the words of the author of the Valaisan quatrains:

Sobs, sobs, pure sobs!
Window, upon which no one leans!
Inconsolable enclosure,
Full of my rain!

It's the too late, the too early
That decides on your forms:
You dress them, curtain,
Dress of emptiness!

If Heinz Julen, the ski instructor, were to reveal a secret to us, it would be that of the love that he bears for his patrimonial family. There are winners only at this game: the customer, the designer, the user, the artisan, the housekeeper, the architecture …

The curtain rises and falls each night at *Vernissage*, at *View House*, at *Loft* – the dance has just begun. I have already caught a glimpse of your next work, Heinz Julen, unlike the previous ones, yet recognisable; it already has that family likeness …

To your next project, Heinz!

---

1 Translator's note: This is a slightly abbreviated translation of the French original.
2 VALERY Paul, Cahiers, Volumes 1&2, Encyclopédie de la Pléiade, Gallimard, Paris, 1973,1974
3 the meaning that is given to it by Paul VIRILIO in *Esthétique de la disparition*
4 Translator's note: the French "chant" (song) and "champ" (field) are homophones.
5 BABELON Jean-Pierre and CHASTEL André, *La notion de patrimoine*, in *Revue de l'Art*, n°49, 1980, Liana Levi, 1995

IDEOLOGIE UND METHODE
ANMERKUNGEN ZU DEN WERKEN VON HEINZ JULEN

CHRISTOPH PARADE

In Anbetracht der grossen Anzahl trostloser Bauten landauf, landab sind Heinz Julens Werke weit mehr als vordergründige, architektonische Umsetzungen funktionaler Belange. Seine Bauten sind die Umsetzung der Visionen eines Künstlers in die dritte Dimension.

Bei der konsequenten Berücksichtigung künstlerischer Belange ist es nur folgerichtig, dass Heinz Julen nicht nur die üblicherweise als bewährt geltenden Wege und Vorgehensweisen immer wieder hinterfragt, sondern infolgedessen auch neue Materialien miteinbeziehen und traditionell bekannte, in Vergessenheit geratene Baustoffe wieder entdeckt.

Dabei beinhaltet sein künstlerisches Konzept, dass sich Materialien natürlicherweise im Laufe der Zeit verändern können. Bewusst lässt er das Altern von Werkstoffen zu, ja, er provoziert es sogar. Man findet in seinen Bauten ausgebleichtes Holz, wie man es von Berghütten kennt; es gehört ebenso zu seinem Repertoire wie der leichte Rostfilm auf Stahlfenstern. Dabei stellt er bewusst einen Gegensatz her zu jenen Bauten, die, dem momentanen gesellschaftlichen Trend entsprechend, alles Altern vertuschen wollen.

In seiner künstlerischen Freiheit weicht er wiederum auch an anderer Stelle ab vom Gewohnten: Mit den mattglänzenden Edelstahlzargen bei einem Restaurant, eingelassen in das rohbehauene Natursteinmauerwerk, bringt er zwar völlig verschiedene Materialien zusammen, er erzielt damit aber auch eine ganz neue Wirkung und zwingt zur Auseinandersetzung mit dem Material: Heinz Julen will «bewusst machen».

Aus diesem Anliegen heraus ist es zu erklären, dass er z.B. den Haupteingang zu seinem Hotelprojekt INTO völlig anders als üblich ausführen liess. Statt der bekannten Zugänge, die eher an einen verbreiteten Büroflur erinnern, schaffte er einen Zuweg, in dem man den Berg spürt. Anstelle glatter Wände, teilweise roh belassener Fels, an dem man noch die Spuren des Presslufthammers ablesen kann.

Auch für die in einem solchen Stollen immer wieder auftretenden Wassertropfen hat er eine Lösung parat: Soweit sie nicht ohnehin direkt verdunsten und somit zur Klimaverbesserung beitragen, werden sie in eine sichtbar belassene Rinne eingeleitet. Vom gedanklichen Ansatz her stellt dies keine Notlösung dar, sondern ist Teil eines ganzheitlichen Konzeptes, eine sinnliche Bereicherung. Man befindet sich eben «im Berg».

Sehr bewusst hat er hier ein Gefühl der Schwere, der Enge zugelassen. Und sicherlich werden bei manchen auch Erinnerungen an Bergwerksstollen wach, die man noch von den obligatorischen Besuchen aus der Schulzeit her kennt. Das Eintauchen in den Berg wird durch eine spezielle Lichtinszenierung noch verstärkt.

Ganz im Gegensatz hierzu, nach Verlassen der «Höhle», der völlig andere Charakter der darüberliegenden Räume: Helligkeit, freier Blick, Leichtigkeit der Konstruktion, Verknüpfung mit der Natur, helle Farben dominieren. Das bewusste Spiel mit den Gegensätzen wird hier wieder sichtbar. Die dadurch entstehende Spannung macht einen Teil der Raumqualität aus: hell – dunkel, grob – fein, hoch – tief, laut – leise, Enge – Weite, Bewegung – Stille… Sie verleiht den Räumen Lebensqualität.

Konsequent wird dieser Gedanke auch im Aussenbereich des Hotels fortgesetzt. Die spitze, weit auskragende Terrasse ist ein gut sichtbares Zeichen – und ein Anstoss zum Nachdenken.

Im Bemühen, völlig Unterschiedliches zusammen zu bringen, integrierte Heinz Julen eine ausrangierte Seilbahn in eine Schmuckboutique. Dabei wurde diese Kabine nicht einfach blind übernommen, sondern ergänzt und verfremdet durch weitere, eigens entwickelte Details. Das Zusammenwirken von edlem Schmuck und Elementen aus der industriellen Produktion war ein eye-catcher. Ein Problem ergab sich allerdings, als der Schmuckladen als ein Verkaufsdepot für Kleider umgenutzt wurde. Denn mit einer neuen, anderen Nutzung kann der künstlerische Ansatz entscheidend geschwächt werden.

Heinz Julens Werke leben von der Gegensätzlichkeit. Das Zusammenfügen vorhandener, alter Fundstücke mit neuen, zeitgemässen Materialien ist kennzeichnend für viele von Julens Arbeiten. Die Verfremdung und die dadurch entstehende Neuinterpretation ist ihm ein Anliegen. Hierbei beschränkt sich Julen nicht nur auf kleinere Objekte. Die Rettung der alten Stahlüberdachung des Zermatter Bahnhofs vor der völligen Zerstörung und deren Wiederverwendung an anderer Stelle sind auch ein Beispiel für sein Bemühen, Geschichte zu erhalten, sichtbar zu machen.

Beim Bau der *Vernissage* geht er ähnliche Wege. Alte Wände und Decken aus abgerissenen Bauernhäusern stellt er in moderne Räume aus Beton. Dies aber wiederum nicht so, dass vollständige Einrichtungen einfach übernommen und an anderer Stelle wieder aufgebaut werden. Er verfremdet Teile des Betons und inszeniert mit gebrauchten Materialien Räume, die das Flair des Alten haben, ohne sich dem Modernen zu verweigern. Der Geruch der gelagerten, wiederverwendeten Materialien, der Duft des Holzes aus dem zum Teil verglasten modernen Kamin bewirken eine Aufenthaltsqualität, die vielen modernen Bauten fehlt.

Die Reihe der künstlerischen Beiträge in diesem Gebäude lässt sich fortsetzen. Sofas, Tische oder Stühle sind scheinbar alt, aber bei näherem Hinsehen aus Altem neu zusammengesetzt und neu interpretiert. Eine geniale Verbindung von Altem und Neuen.

In der Materialausbildung entsprechen manche Details sicherlich nicht den akademischen Vorgaben, welche an Architekturhochschulen gelehrt werden und sicherlich auch wichtig sind. Aber Heinz Julen ist einen anderen Weg gegangen. Seine Ansätze für Problemlösungen sind unbelastet von Baunormen oder Vorurteilen, die durchaus hinderlich für Neuentwicklungen sein können.

In diesem Zusammenhang sind die architektonischen Konzepte seiner Ateliers besonders interessant: Eines davon befindet sich auf 2100 Metern über Meer. Ein einziger Raum, aus dem Material der bestehenden Berghütten erbaut, aber in seiner Zusammenstellung ein Novum. Die Hütte fügt sich in ihre Umgebung ein, ohne sich unterzuordnen.

Im zweiten Atelier, im Ort Zermatt selbst, macht der Umgang mit Baustoffen, wie Beton, Glas und Holz, angesichts der vorherrschenden Chalet- Ästhetik eine neue Aussage. Aussen und Innen wirken aufgrund der grossen Glaswand als Einheit. Der roh belassene, glatte Beton der Wände, konsequent fortgeführt bis hin zur Ausbildung des Fussbodens, verleiht dem Raum Ursprünglichkeit. Dagegen gesetzt: Glas mit feinen Profilen aus Holz, z.T. eingefasst in mattglänzende Stahlrahmen. Besonders erwähnenswert ist der aussen – statt innen – angebrachte Vorhang entlang der gesamten riesigen Glasfront. Aussenjalousien sind zwar längst bekannt, aber automatisch regulierbare Vorhänge in ca. 90 cm Abstand von der Fassade sind eine Neuheit. Statt des gewohnten innen liegenden Vorhangs wellt sich der weisse Stoff, immer dem Wind entsprechend; die sanfte Bewegung des Stoffes verleiht dem Raum Sinnlichkeit.

Der künstlerische Impuls ist in jedem seiner Werke zu erkennen. Fürs *View House* hat Heinz Julen neue Möbel entworfen und sich, bis hin zum Ausgussbecken, nicht nur Lösungen erdacht, sondern sich auch über konstruktive Details Gedanken gemacht. Dieser gedankliche Ansatz wird im Hotelbau *INTO* konsequent fortgesetzt.

In diesem Gebäude befinden sich Ideen, die vom bisher Vertrauten völlig abweichen. Er verzichtet auf jene gängigen Details, die in Varianten in allen internationalen Hotels auftauchen. Durch andere gedankliche Ansätze kommt er zu völlig neuen Lösungen. Heinz Julen möchte, neben Aufenthaltsqualität, auch Erinnerungswert schaffen. Denn sie ist letztlich Grund für den Besucher, an diesen Ort zurückzukehren.

Eine Bar, die sich als Hubboden über mehrere Geschosse bewegt – und damit alle wesentlichen Ebenen verbindet – gab es bisher noch nie. Mit der sichtbar belassenen Konstruktion des Hubbodens, den Zahnrädern, Schrauben und Schweissstellen weicht er ab vom Üblichen; man sieht die Bewegung, das Ineinandergreifen der Zahnräder. Das Auf und Ab der Bar wird zum Event. Auch wenn dies für manche übertrieben wirken mag, der Eindruck des Aussergewöhnlichen, des Einmaligen bleibt bestehen.

Das Aneinanderreihen von Überraschungen setzt sich im Speisesaal fort. Von den Sesseln (ein Entwurf von Heinz Julen) bis den Tischen erinnert nichts an Gewohntes. Unter der Glasplatte im Boden des Speisesaals kann man ein Wasserbecken entdecken, welches durch ausgefeilte Technik innert Minuten in ein offenliegendes

Sprudelbecken verwandelt werden kann. Wo sich vorher die Glasplatte befand, findet sich nun auf gleicher Höhe, inmitten der Tische, ein Wasserspiel. Das Geräusch wirkt beruhigend und entspannend beim Speisen.

Glas – Durchblicke und Einblicke spielen bei diesem Gebäude eine ganz besondere Rolle. Treppen und Flurböden aus Glas vermitteln Transparenz und Leichtigkeit. Die Balkonböden aus Glas sind ebenfalls Teil dieser Konzeption, die Transparenz und bessere Lichtausbeute in den Zimmern anstrebt.

Bei der Ausgestaltung des Schlafbereiches nimmt Heinz Julen den Trend auf, Schlaf- und Badebereiche stärker zu verbinden. Der gesamte Raum wird zum Wellnessbereich, die schwarze, beheizte Betonbadewanne als Skulptur inmitten des Raumes ist Teil dieser Idee. Das drehbare Doppelbett mit dem in die Fensterfront eingelassenen Fernsehgerät ist ein Zeichen des Bemühens, Wohn- und Erlebniswert zu erhöhen.

Der ausfahrbare Pool in der Präsidentensuite ist schliesslich ein ganz besonderer Beitrag. Bei geöffneter Kuppel schwebt man über den Dächern von Zermatt, wie in einem Vogelnest. Man spürt dabei unversehens ein Gefühl der Freiheit, des Gelöstseins, des Einmaligen. Man hebt ab.

Im Gegensatz hierzu das halboffene Bad, sichtbar dem Eingangsfoyer zugeordnet. Mit seinen schwarzen, geschliffenen Granitplatten und dem in Edelstahl ausgeführten Pool hat es etwas Magisches. Die harten Materialien werden ausgeglichen durch die spielerische Gestaltung der grossen, glitzernden, formenreichen Kronleuchtern (vom Künstler selbst entworfen). Wiederum sind es die Gegensätze und die Andersartigkeit der Materialkombinationen – z.B. von handelsüblichen Perlketten, wie sie an Stöpseln von Waschbecken zu finden sind, mit chromglänzenden Abflussrohren, mit verfremdeten Tafelbesteck usw. –, welche die Atmosphäre ausmachen.

Sie verleihen dem Raum eine augenzwinkernde Feierlichkeit.

Diese Innovationen setzen sich im ganzen Gebäude fort, von der Discobar bis hin zur herunterklappbaren Leinwand.

Bedingt durch die Durchblicke, die Transparenz und die räumlichen Überraschungen ist ein Hotel entstanden, welches dem Bedürfnis nach Einmaligkeit sehr entgegenkommt.

Vieles scheint nicht von vornherein geplant worden zu sein: Es ist vor Ort entstanden, und dies ist gerade ein Teil des Konzeptes von Heinz Julen. Sicherlich ein Nachteil für jene, die mit fixfertigen Plänen, ohne jegliches Risiko ein Haus errichten wollten. Doch jeder, der baut, weiss, dass vor Ort vieles anders aussieht, und man vieles während des Bauablaufs ändern möchte (und müsste). Das Arbeiten und Weiterentwickeln vor Ort ist Teil von Julens Arbeitsweise. Er verzichtet darauf, seine eigenen Ideen computergesteuert auf Glanzpapier zu präsentieren. Zu seiner Vorgehensweise am Bau gehört die Entscheidung auf der Baustelle, notfalls auch die letzte Ausarbeitung auf einem Stück Butterbrotpapier.

Dadurch dass Heinz Julen oft kleinste Baudetails künstlerisch ausformt und verfremdet, unterscheidet er sich in seinen architektonischen Aussagen wesentlich vom herkömmlichen Bauen. Mit viel Witz und Einfällen schafft er ein Ambiente, das man sonst nur von alten Gebäuden kennt. Und man wird immer wieder gehalten, über den Ursprung dieser Arbeit und der verwendeten Materialien nachzudenken.

Vor keinem Detail scheint Heinz Julens Denken Halt zu machen. Sein Entwurf für einen zusammenklappbaren, rollbaren Schreibtisch zeigt, dass er sich mit der Funktion kleinster Elemente befasst. Die Möglichkeit, diesen Schreibtisch in Sekundenschnelle in eine versandfähige Kiste umzugestalten, entspricht dem Mobilitätsdrang der heutigen Zeit.

Es gehört zur vernetzten Denkweise von Heinz Julen, dass er die energetischen Probleme in seine Bauten und Werke einbezieht. Die Nutzung von Solarenergie und Erdwärme im *View House* sind nur zwei Beispiele.

Das Infragestellen und Verlassen konventioneller Regeln, eingefahrener Trassen, welche interessanterweise gerade bei herausragenden Architekten bis zum heutigen Tage regelmässig vorkommen, ist, wie die Geschichte beweist, immer wieder ein Anstoss zum Umdenken. Dies fördert die bauliche Entwicklung gleichermassen wie das Bewahren tradierter Details.

Solche Einsicht ist nicht nur begrenzt auf grosse architektonische Beiträge, sondern setzt sich bis in kleinste Einzelheiten – wie bei den Bauten von Heinz Julen zu erkennen ist – fort. Seine architektonischen Beiträge sind eine Aufforderung zur Auseinandersetzung mit dem Gewohnten. Durch seine eigenwillige Interpretation zeigt er Wege auf, über die es sich lohnt zu diskutieren. Ein Anstoss, zu dem viele Architekten, eingeengt durch Normen und Vorgaben, kaum noch in der Lage sind.

Da durch die Eigenwilligkeit von Heinz Julen Konfliktstoff bereits programmiert ist, sind seine Werke sehr bereichernd. Diese Architektur mit herkömmlichen Mitteln und Kriterien beurteilen zu wollen, wäre ein falscher Ansatz. Seine Beiträge sind «das Salz in der Suppe» einer unhinterfragten Normen folgenden Bautechnik. Kunstbauwerke wie jene von Heinz Julen durch behördliche Auflagen generell zu verhindern, würde zu einer Verarmung der Architektur führen. Für die Schweiz, die durch ihre exzellenten architektonischen Leistungen weltweit immer wieder Aufsehen erregt, wäre dies von grossem Nachteil. Es wäre ein kultureller Verlust.

IDEOLOGY AND METHOD
SOME NOTES ON WORKS BY HEINZ JULEN

CHRISTOPH PARADE

Compared with the large majority of dismal buildings all over the country, Heinz Julen's works are much more than the obvious architectural realisation of functional needs. His structures are three-dimensional realisations of his artistic vision and, as such, he consistently takes into consideration his artistic concerns. Hence, it is logical, not only that he should keep questioning generally approved approaches and methods, but also that he should continually try new materials and revive traditional ones that have fallen into disuse.

His artistic concept also accepts that materials may change naturally over time, as they age. He intentionally allows materials to age; occasionally, he will even emphasize the process. Some of his buildings contain weathered wood such as one might find in alpine cabins; aging is as much a part of his repertoire as is a film of rust on his steel windows, for example. In this, he quite deliberately places himself in opposition to the current social trend which attempts to conceal any traces of aging. He also takes artistic liberties in other respects: in a restaurant, for example, where he inserted dully gleaming stainless frames into a wall built of rough-hewn natural rock, he not only combined completely different materials, but also achieved a completely new effect, forcing us to think about his use of materials. In other words, Heinz Julen wants to "raise our awareness."

This concern of his also explains why, in his *INTO the hotel* project, he designed the main entrance in a completely novel way. Rather than the usual entrance, which tends to be reminiscent of a somewhat wider hallway in an office, he created an entryway that made one feel the presence of the mountain. Instead of smooth walls, there was live rock still bearing the scars of the jackhammer. He even had an answer to the problem of the dripping water that tends to seep into such galleries: some of it would evaporate naturally, improving the air; the rest was evacuated in visible gutters. In Julen's concept, this is not a compromise, but part of the bigger plan, a sensorial enhancement, emphasizing the fact that one is underground, "in the pit," as it were. In this situation, the artist most deliberately allowed for an atmosphere of heaviness, of constriction. Many visitors were doubtless reminded of mining shafts they might have had to visit on a school excursion. The impression of entering the mountain was further enhanced by special lighting effects.

What a contrast provided by the rooms above this "cave": there was bright light, the eye roamed freely, structures were light, there was again a close link with nature, and bright colours dominated. Again, the deliberate play on contrasts, a tension which was part of the quality of the rooms: dark – bright, coarse – smooth, low – high, loud – silent, constriction – freedom, stillness – movement … All this instilled the rooms with a life-enhancing atmosphere. Julen was consistent in carrying this concept through in the exterior as well. The pointed sundeck that jutted far into the village was a clearly visible sign, as well as a stimulus for reflection.

In his attempt to combine completely disparate elements, Julen integrated the disused gondola of a cable railway into a jewelry shop. However, he did not leave it as it was, but added specially designed details, creating an alienation effect. The conjunction of delicate jewelry and elements from industrial production was an eye-catcher. A problem arose, however, when the jewelry shop became an outlet for clothes: the altered use crucially weakened the artistic statement.

Heinz Julen's works depend on contrasts. The combination of available, found objects with new, contemporary materials is characteristic of many of his works. He is interested in the alienation effect and the resulting re-interpretation. He applies his concept not only to smaller objects. For example, he saved the old steel roof of the Zermatt railway station from being scrapped, and used it elsewhere. This, too, is proof of his endeavor to preserve history and make it visible.

His approach to *Vernissage* was similar. In modern rooms made of concrete, he installed old walls and ceilings salvaged from doomed farmhouses. Again, he did not simply transfer complete interiors, but rather alienated parts of the concrete, and visibly created spaces with used materials, such that the rooms are inspired by the old without rejecting the new. The smell of long-stored, recycled materials, the fragrance of wood from the partially-glazed, modern fireplace produce a comfort-level that is missing from many other modern buildings. The list of Julen's artistic contributions to this location continues: sofas, tables, and chairs look old, but on closer inspection are recompositions of old materials, producing a modern reinterpretation, an inspired combination of old and new.

With regard to Julen's use of materials, some details certainly do not correspond to the admittedly important academic norms taught at schools of architecture. He has adopted a different route. His solutions often blithely disregard building regulations or prejudices that may impede new developments. In this context, his architectural ideas for his studios are of particular interest: one of them is located at an altitude of 2,100 m above sea-level. It is a single room, made of the same materials as mountain cabins elsewhere, but composed in a novel way; the cabin fits into the existing pattern without subordinating itself. In Julen's second studio, a loft in the village of Zermatt, where the "chalet aesthetic" is predominant, his treatment of materials such as concrete, glass and wood makes a bold, new statement: a large glass front merges interior with exterior. The untreated, smooth concrete, in both the walls and the floor, lends naturalness to the room. The concrete is contrasted with glass combined with delicate wooden profiles, or set into dully gleaming steel frames. A particularly noteworthy feature is the curtain across the entire, huge glass front – mounted outside rather than inside. While exterior blinds have long been in use, automatically adjustable curtains set approx. 90 cm away from the façade are a novelty. The white fabric ripples in the wind, and its gentle motion lends a sensual element to the room.

Julen's artistic impulse is reflected in each one of his works. For *View House*, he not only designed new furniture, but also created a new design for the kitchen sink, as well as other structural novelties.

This conceptual approach found its logical extension in Julen's *INTO the hotel*. This building contained new solutions that were a total departure from existing architecture. Approaching the task from a completely different angle, he avoided the commonplace details of virtually all international hotels. His intention was not only to ensure that the patrons had a pleasant stay, but that their visit was to be an unforgettable experience. Their unique memory was to be one of the chief reasons why people would return.

One of the new elements was a bar on a platform that could be raised and lowered across several floors, connecting the most important levels. The platform's structural elements, all the cog-wheels, bolts, screws, and welding seams, were exposed – another unusual feature revealing its motion and its workings. Raising and lowering the bar was a spectacular event that some people might have considered over the top, but which made an indelible impression.

The dining room held more surprises, namely the Julen-designed chairs, the unusual tables, the glass-floor across a shimmering pool. Within minutes it could be converted into an open whirlpool and raised to table-top level, producing a dining experience enhanced by the soothing splashing and rippling of water.

Glass, providing transparency and allowing for vistas and glimpses everywhere, played a crucial role. Glass stairs and hallway floors imparted a feeling of weightlessness. The glass floors of the balconies were another part of this concept, and enhanced the lighting of the rooms.

In the design of the sleeping quarters, Julen adopted the current trend of merging bed- and bathroom, creating a "wellness" zone in which the black, heated bathtub in the center made a bold, sculptural statement. The revolving double-bed, the TV set built into the window, etc., were further features that enhanced the comfort-level and novelty-value of the rooms.

The Presidential Suite held the ultimate surprise, an extensible pool. When its dome was open, it felt like a bird's nest, as though one were floating high above the rooftops of Zermatt. The feeling was one of great freedom and relaxation, of being in a totally unique place.

The semi-public pool, an extension of the lobby, came as a stark contrast. There was something darkly magical about its polished black granite slabs and the stainless steel pool. The spare, cold materials were counterbalanced by playful, large chandeliers (another Julen design), exuberant in their multitude of forms and shapes. Each one of them was unique, fashioned from store-bought bead chains, commonly attach to drainhole plugs, and chromium-plated waste pipes, alienated cutlery, etc. Yet again, it is the contrast and difference in materials that created a special atmosphere – in this case, one of slightly mischievous festiveness.

The entire building held more such innovations, ranging from the disco bar to the mobile film screen. In all, the hotel's vistas, transparency and surprising features combined to create a place that truly answered the wish for uniqueness.

Much of what was created at *INTO the hotel* did not seem to have been the result of long-term planning. Rather, it was created on-site, which is part of Julen's concept. This is no doubt inconvenient to those who wish to avoid risks, and prefer to build a house according to tried-and-tested blueprints. As anyone involved in construction knows, however, each site is different, and one would often wish for changes to be made throughout. Indeed, part of Julen's approach is working on-site, developing his project up to the very end, going as far as drawing details on a piece of wax paper, if necessary. He is not one to present his computer-generated designs on glossy paper.

Heinz Julen often adds his alienating artistic touch to the slightest structural details. This makes his architectural statements vastly different from run-of-the-mill architecture. The influence of and inspiration by art can be felt in all his activities, not least as regards his selection, use, and treatment of materials. His whimsical ideas create an atmosphere that is usually common only to old houses. Again and again, one is inspired to reflect on the origin of his works, and of the materials used for them. No detail seems to be too insignificant for Julen's mind. His design for a foldable desk on wheels, for example, shows that he concerns himself with functionality to the last detail. Within seconds, this desk can be converted into a box ready for shipping, a feature that accommodates the current vogue for total mobility.

It is also part of Julen's integrated approach to address the question of how energy is used in his works and buildings, for example the use of solar and geothermal energy in his *View House*.

History has shown that impulses for new ideas often result from the questioning of and disregard for conventional rules and well-trodden paths. Interestingly, this is something that outstanding architects practice frequently. They promote both structural developments and the preservation of traditional details. With regard to Heinz Julen, this principle applies not only to large-scale architectural contributions but, as his buildings demonstrate, continues down to the most minute detail. They are invitations to reconsider that which has long been established. His unconventional interpretations present avenues that merit discussion, and his innovations would well befit many architects too constricted by norms and regulations.

While Heinz Julen's unconventionality provokes conflict, his works are particularly inspiring. It would be wrong to apply traditional criteria when judging his architecture; his contributions are stimuli to construction techniques that no longer question norms. The world of architecture would be impoverished if official norms and regulations were used to impede any such creative architectural designs. It would also be a cultural loss, and a detriment to Switzerland, whose great architectural achievements have stirred the imagination of the world.

EINE BEERDIGUNG ODER: DIE VOLLENDUNG EINER VISION

Nach seinem Ausschluss aus dem *INTO the hotel*-Projekt zieht sich Heinz Julen in sein Bergatelier zurück. Dort malt er Porträts seiner engsten Mitarbeiter. Es handelt sich um seine persönliche Hommage an jene Menschen, die bedingungslos an die *INTO*-Welt geglaubt und diese mitaufgebaut haben: Ingenieure, Elektroplaner, Energiekonzepter, Maschinenbauer, Handwerker, Baukontrolleure, Marketingleute u.v.a.m. Julen fragt die Leute an, und selbstverständlich ziehen sie alle ihr Hemd aus, um sich von ihm porträtieren zu lassen. Auch seinen (ehemaligen) Partner Alexander Schärer und dessen Freundin Marianna will er porträtieren, schliesslich hätte es ohne sie das *INTO* so nicht gegeben; doch da alle Kommunikationswege verbaut sind, kann er sie nicht erreichen. Und so malt er sie, wie er sie in Erinnerung hat.

Alle 30 Porträts hängt Heinz Julen in einem schwarzen Raum auf, den er «Der letzte Raum einer Vision» nennt. Der letzte Raum des *INTO*-Projektes befindet sich ausserhalb des Hotels, da der Künstler inzwischen Hausverbot bekommen hat. Kerzen beleuchten die Porträts; die Installation stellt die Beerdigung der *INTO*-Vision dar.

A FUNERAL, OR: A VISION ACHIEVED

Following his expulsion from *INTO the hotel*, Heinz Julen retires to his mountain studio where he paints the portraits of his closest co-workers. This is his personal homage to those who unconditionally believed in the world of *INTO* and helped create it: civil engineers, electrical designers, electricians, mechanical engineers, craftsmen, building inspectors, marketing specialists, etc., etc.. Julen asks for permission to paint them with a bare chest, and of course they all take off their shirts to be photographed by him. He also wants to paint his (former) partner, Alexander Schärer, and his girlfriend, Marianna – after all, they were instrumental in the creation of *INTO* as it was. However, all avenues of communication having been severed, he can not reach them. He therefore paints their portraits from memory.

Heinz Julen hangs the 30 portraits in a black room which he calles "The Last Room of a Vision". Because the artist has been barred from the hotel, the last room of the *INTO* project is located outside of it. The portraits are lit by candles; the installation symbolizes the burial of the *INTO* vision.

Roberto, Galerist

Willi, Metallbauer

Charly, Maschinenbauer

Manuel, Hilfsarbeiter

Martin, Künstler

Paulo, Schlosser

Irs, Marketing

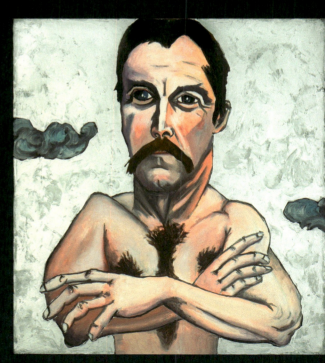

Fredi, Sprengmeister

Gitz, Sanitär

Alex, Unternehmer

Amadée, Elektriker

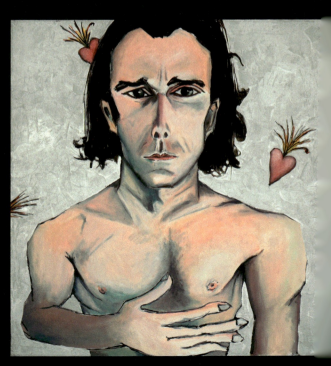

Heinz, Künstler

Marianna, Freundin

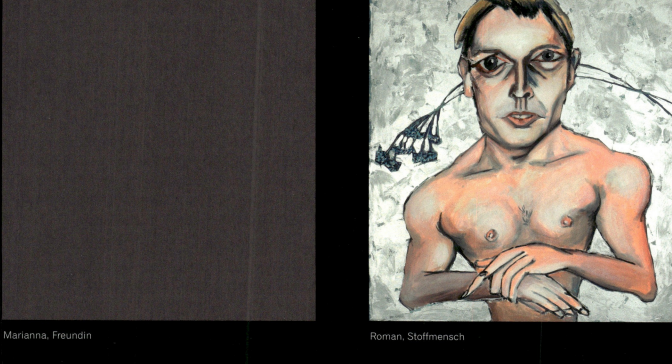

Roman, Stoffmensch

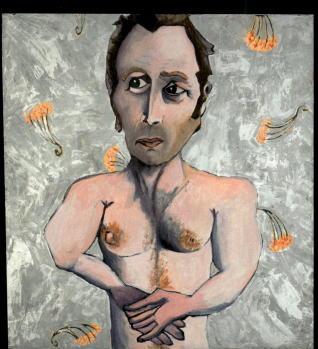

Julius, Rechte Hand

Peter, Energietechniker

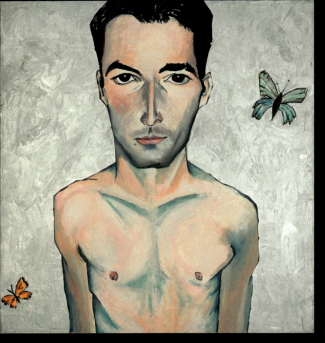

Daniel, Galerist

Balthasar, Künstler

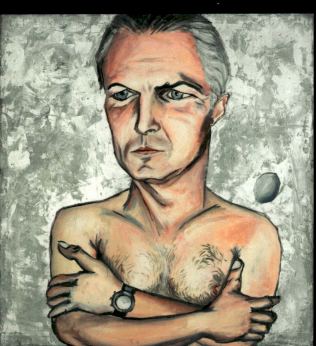

Max, Analytiker

Sarni, Bauleiter / Baufachmann

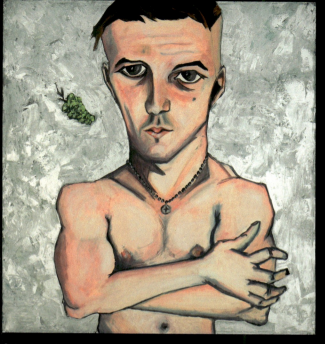
Sebastian, Schreiner

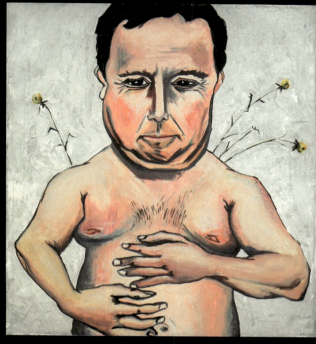
Fiori, Spengler

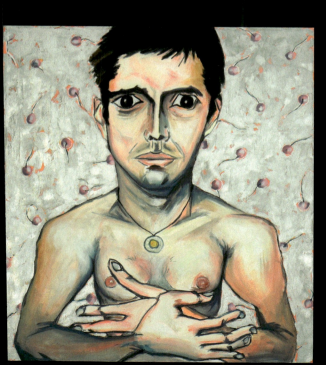
olf, Wellness-Konzepter

Christian, Texter

Peter, Konstrukteur

Poli, Architekt

José, Hilfsarbeiter

Roli, Sanitär

Sarbach, Baumeister

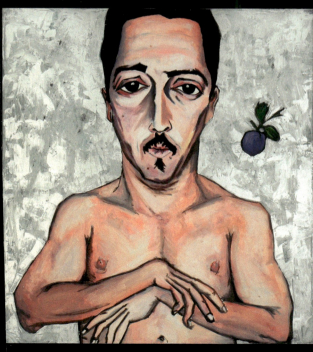

Augustino, Allrounder

... UND DIE LINKE WANGE   «Der letzte Raum einer Vision» wird an der *Kunst 2000* in Zürich gezeigt, dann in Zermatt, von wo Alexander Schärer und seine Freundin Marianna Bilski ihre beiden Porträts gerichtlich aus der Installation entfernen lassen. Bei der Zeugeneinvernahme vor Gericht im Frühling 2002 fallen Anschuldigungen wie «morbid», «homoerotisch», «pornographische Situation»; es werden Verwandtschaften zum Dritten Reich moniert, «Nazimachenschaften», «Goebbels Manieren». Zudem habe, so der Vorwurf, der Künstler Marianna eine zu lange Nase gemalt – interpretiert wird dies von der Klägerpartei als bewusster Hinweis auf Mariannas jüdische Abstammung; Verbindungen zur Judenverfolgung und -vergasung im Dritten Reich werden gezogen.

Heinz Julen als Angeklagter vor dem Richter: «Ich weiss, dass es jedem Menschen frei steht, Dinge zu interpretieren, frei bleibt, sich seine eigene Welt zu schaffen, sie so zu sehen wie er sie sehen will. Diese harten Vorwürfe sprechen eine Sprache, die ich nie verstehen werde.»

... AND THE LEFT CHEEK   "The Last Room of a Vision" is shown at *Kunst 2000* in Zürich before it is moved to Zermatt, where Alexander Schärer and his girlfriend, Marianna Bilski, obtain a court-order to have their portraits removed from the installation. In spring 2002, when witnesses are called to testify in court, accusations are voiced; terms such as "morbid", "homoerotic", "pornographic situation" are used; complaints are made about conditions resembling the Third Reich, "Nazi machinations" and "Goebbels-like behaviour". Moreover, the artist is accused of painting Marianna with a nose that is too long – the plaintiffs interpret this as a conscious allusion to her Jewish background; parallels are drawn to the persecution and gassing of Jews in the Third Reich.

Heinz Julen, the defendant, tells the judge, "I know that everyone is free in their interpretation, free to create their own world, to see it as they please. These harsh accusations are expressed in a language that I will never understand."

EIN HIMMELBLAUER BALKON
ODER: EINIGE GEDANKEN ZUM WERK VON HEINZ JULEN

CORNELIA PROVIDOLI

I   Drei weisse Lavabos stehen mitten im Dorf auf einem Gestänge. Wenn man von der Hauptstrasse, die den Bahnhof direkt mit der Dorfkirche verbindet, ungefähr auf halbem Weg links abzweigt und gegen die Migros und die dahinter liegenden Tennisplätze zugeht, steht da plötzlich am linken Strassenrand ein Objekt. Wasser sprudelt aus allen Hähnen bis die Becken voll sind und dann überlaufen, über den Rand des glimmernden Porzellans und über die bereits rostigen Rohre auf den Boden – Tropfen für Tropfen. In eine kleine Messingplatte ist ein Name *Heinz Julen* und eine Jahreszahl *1993* eingestanzt. Dazu steht *Überfluss*.

II   Gegen elf Uhr morgens verlasse ich das Dorf in Richtung Findeln. Die Sonne brennt auf die braunen Dächer, die sich geduckt um die Kirche scharen. Aufgeregt zirpen die Grillen im zittrigen Gras, die Vögel zwitschern matt im Gebüsch. Von weit her bimmeln die Pferdekutschen und Elektromobile, nur durch den unterschiedlichen Rhythmus voneinander unterscheidbar, und weiter unten im Dorf herrscht emsiges Treiben. Ich erspähe die rote Zahnradeisenbahn, wie sie mühsam von Täsch her die letzten Kurven erklimmt und endlich langsam in den Bahnhof findet, wieder eine Ladung Gäste aus ihrem Bauch und in das Dorf entlassend, und die Hoteliers im Bergdorf sind in guter Stimmung. Weiss blitzen die Tischtücher in der Mittagssonne und stramm stehen die Kellner vor den braungebrannten Fenstersimsen, derweil heiteres Lachen aus den verstaubten Hinterhöfen in die Dorfstrasse perlt. Es ist ein hochsommerlicher Tag. Corinna hätte sich gefreut und schwarze Erdbeeren gepflückt.

III   Heinz Julen, am 29. Februar 1964 als zweites von vier Kindern in Zermatt geboren, beginnt sich ab seinem sechzehnten Lebensjahr nachhaltig mit dem Schaffen von Kunstgegenständen auseinanderzusetzen und unternimmt auch erste malerische Versuche. Nach dem Besuch des einjährigen Vorkurses an der *Ecole cantonale des Beaux-Arts* in Sitten kehrt er ins heimatliche Dorf zurück und fängt an, ein selbständiges gestalterisches Vokabular zu formulieren. Dabei zieht er fast sämtliche Register des Gattungskanons, er malt, kreiert Skulpturen und Objekte, entwickelt Möbel und Gebrauchsgegenstände, veranstaltet Aktionen und Happenings in der freien Natur, die er mit Foto und Video dokumentiert. Darüber hinaus konzipiert er Ausstellungsräume und programmiert ein Kulturzentrum.

Geistesverwandt mit den Künstlern der Renaissance versteht Heinz Julen die Architektur als eigentliche Königin der Disziplinen. Seine künstlerische Vision gilt der Schaffung einer eigenen Welt, einer Art Gesamtkunstwerk, das er bis in die kleinsten Details selbst entwerfen und im besten Fall auch realisieren kann. Seine Kreativität ist eingebettet in einer tiefen Spiritualität und einer religiös motivierten Weltauffassung, die im katholischen Glauben wurzelt. In seinem Schaffen setzt er sich mit den formalen Bedingungen eines gegebenen Zweckes auseinander. Die Formen, die er findet, folgen Funktionen. Ihn interessiert das Gebrauchsmoment (the urgent moment) als Ausgangspunkt seiner Arbeit.

Er lässt Schwachstellen im System zu, und würde sogar bewusst solche inszenieren, um einen Schritt näher zum Wesentlichen, zum Kern vorzustossen, um Erkenntnis zu erlangen. Er schafft mobile, fragile Welten, wo alles immer anders kommen kann, als es ursprünglich gedacht war.

Zu seinen architektonisch wichtigsten Projekten können der Bau des *Bergateliers Findeln* 1980 und dessen Umbau 1989 gezählt werden. Ausserdem die Konzeption, Planung und Realisation des Kulturzentrums Vernissage, das 1992 eröffnet wurde. Der im Dorfkern von Zermatt liegende dreistöckige, zum Teil unterirdische Bau beherbergt neben einer Bar, einem Kino und einer Konzertbühne auch eine Galerie für zeitgenössische Kunst, die *Kunsträume Zermatt*. Julens Vision, einen Ort zu kreieren, wo verschiedene Raumfunktionen und Nutzungen sich überlappen, ja sogar durch eigens entwickelte technische oder mechanische Vorrichtungen den wechselnden Bedürfnissen der Besucher innert Sekunden sanft angepasst werden können, findet in diesem Bau erstmals umfängliche Anwendung. Die wunderbaren Leuchter im Kinoraum schwingen nach dem Ende der Vorstellungen surrend an ihren Ort im Zentrum des Saales zurück, während sie vor den Filmvorführungen weg von der Mitte an den Rand der Kulissen gefahren werden. Jean Tinguely und seine kinetischen Skulpturen aus Abfall grüssen. Heinz entwirft das gesamte Möbelinventar für das Haus selbst und setzt damit ein Statement für seine Leidenschaft für das Möbel- und Produkte-Design. Seit seinen ersten künstlerischen Schritten kreiert Heinz Julen eigene Möbel. Sie sind mobile Module, die je nach Bedürfnis ergänzt oder angepasst werden können. 1995 definiert er das Cube System und präsentiert es 1996 bei Möbel Strebel AG in Aarau und in der Kornschütte Luzern. 1993/1994, beginnt der Bau des *View-House*, ein Apartmenthaus, das an Feriengäste vermietet wird. 1997 installiert er eine mobile Bar im Restaurant Affenkasten in Aarau. Ebenfalls 1997 beginnt Heinz Julen mit den Planungsarbeiten zu seinem bis anhin komplexesten Kunstwerk, dem *INTO the hotel*-Projekt. Am 29.2.2000 offiziell eröffnet, wird es 7 Wochen später wieder geschlossen.

INTO war sein Traum – dort sah er die Möglichkeit der vollkommenen Realisation seiner Ideen. Heinz trieb sein Konzept der mobilen Vernetzung von Räumen und deren möglichen Nutzungen weiter voran. Wundersame technische Erfindungen verwandelten das Hotel in ein magisches Perpetuum Mobile, das sich chamäleonartig den erforderlichen Bedürfnissen entsprechend verändern und anpassen konnte. Als neues Moment im Ganzen bekam im *INTO the hotel* eine bislang eher latent mitschwingende Seite in Heinz Julens Werk zum ersten Mal eine bewusst konzeptuelle Prägung: sein Interesse für soziale Abläufe und Regeln. Er versuchte durch eine Umkehrung der Welt existente Muster aufzubrechen und neu zu durchmischen. Er vermittelte andere Werte, schuf Orte und Plätze für geistige, spirituelle und auch sinnliche Anregungen. Dies geschah in absolutem Einklang und oft auch gerade mit Unterstützung seiner fluktuierenden Architekturmodule. Die hundert Angestellten des Hotelbetriebes waren voll in den Fertigstellungsprozess des Hotels eingebunden und packten ungeachtet ihrer ursprünglichen Funktion mit an. Die Arbeitsfläche war zugleich auch Erholungsfläche und umgekehrt. Heinz beschrieb seine Idee des Bar-Moduls folgendermassen: "*INTO the bar*, Ort des schnellen Beisammensitzens, der Abwechslung, ein kleines Zwischenstück, ein Zeitvertreib. Auf einer runden, im Durchmesser fünf Meter grossen Metallplatte angelegt, um sich auf drei verschiedene Stockwerke verschieben zu lassen. Je nach Tageszeit folgte sie den Bedürfnissen der Menschen und passte sich räumlich an. Am Morgen weit oben, wo die Sonne die Terrasse und die Eingangshalle am meisten streifte. Mittags ein Stück tiefer bei der Lounge, oder bei Bedarf beim Pool. Auf der Ausstellungs- oder Speisesaal-Ebene abends. *INTO the bar* war ‹Schrankenbrecherin› zwischen den Dienenden und den Bedienten und nur erreichbar durch das Aufheben des persönlichen Bereiches, der Arbeitsfläche der Dienenden. Die Bar sollte Ort, Familie aller dort arbeitenden und wohnenden Menschen werden."

IV Die ältere Schwester betreibt in Findeln unterhalb des Bergateliers seit geraumer Zeit ein Restaurant. Hier ist Heinz mit seinen drei Schwestern aufgewachsen und verbrachte er den grössten Teil seiner Kindheit. Auf dem Weg durchs Haus kann der Gast Wände übersät mit Familienfotos entdecken. Schwarz-weisse und bunte Aufnahmen dicht aneinander. Sie zeigen vier kleine Kinder und die Eltern. Glück, Liebe, Wärme und Harmonie ist in allen möglichen Situationen auf Zelluloid festgehalten. Dazwischen liebevoll arrangierte Blumensträusse, auf hölzernen Tischlein. Stühle auf Steinplatten. Das Holzkreuz. Und immer wieder die Natur und der eindrückliche Berg, das Matterhorn. Das Haus atmet Geschichte und beseelte Erinnerung. Hier liegt der Kern.

V Martin und Julie sind bereits da als ich auf der Alp ankomme. Es ist jetzt kurz nach ein Uhr. Sie sitzen draussen auf der hölzernen Terrasse und trinken ein Glas kühlen Weisswein. Es ist Montag und einzelne Spuren erzählen von einem mit Freunden verbrachten Wochenende, die offenbar während des Vormittages abgereist sind. Nur noch Martin und Julie sind da. Ich freue mich. Martin kenne ich bereits von Zürich, aber Julie hatte ich noch nie getroffen. Auf die Frage nach seinen künstlerischen und baulichen Anfängen greift Heinz schmunzelnd auf die Geschichte mit seinem Vater zurück, dem er als Halbwüchsiger beim Umbau von alten Walliserhäusern zur Hand ging. Ausserdem habe er als kleiner Bub in Findeln Hütten aus Tüchern, Fellen, alten Holzstücken und Stangen gebaut und seine Schwestern zum Tee eingeladen: "Als kleines Kind hoch oben in den Bergen fing ich an, Hütten zu bauen, diese wurden immer besser, plötzlich überlebten sie gar die schweren Wintermonate. Und ich war stolz, habe sie dekoriert, ihnen Leben eingehaucht, Stimmungen geschaffen und lud meine drei Schwestern zum Nächtigen dort ein. Ich war ein Kind, beflügelt und getragen vom Geschaffenen, und meinen Schwestern hat es gefallen. Und immer entwickelte ich mich weiter, weiter in meiner Welt. Der Welt der

Konstruktionen, der Erfahrungen und Möglichkeiten. Und nie habe ich diesen Weg gestoppt. Nie habe ich ihn abgebrochen. Nie wollte ich es anders tun. Nein, ich baute mich ein in meine, mir ganz eigen gewordene Sprache und immer mehr Leute wollten sie lesen und leben."

Heinz sitzt jetzt im Adlerhorst und zeichnet. Später wird er das Gezeichnete selber umsetzen und bauen, er vermisst und rechnet. In meiner Erinnerung bleibt der grosse Bürotisch übersät von unzähligen Zeichnungen und Papier, die steilen Stufen hinauf in den Ort der Erfindung und der Tüftelei. Ein Labor und eine Experimentierkammer. Riesige Glasscheiben anstelle von Wänden im Schöpfungscockpit, das aus dem offenen Dach dem klaren Himmel entgegenwächst und den Nachdenkenden scheinbar nahtlos in das Universum einbindet.

Später fahren Martin und Julie mit der Bahn runter ins Dorf. Heinz erzählt. Da ist sein Traum von der totalen Integration der Kunst in den Alltag. Er sieht eine Herausforderung darin, für die Kunst immer wieder experimentelle Plattformen zu finden: Seine erste Ausstellung hatte er als Teenager im Keller einer Kleiderboutique in Zermatt; den Keller habe er gleich zu einer Galerie umgebaut. Einige Jahre später schleppte er seine Skulpturen und Objekte, die im Bergatelier entstanden waren, auf verschiedene Berggipfel in der näheren Umgebung. Eine Aktion, die er mit Foto- und Filmaufnahmen dokumentierte. 1990 kann er anlässlich des internationalen Damen-Tennisturniers in Zürich vor Ort seine Arbeiten in einer Ausstellung präsentieren. Von der Tages-Anzeiger-Gruppe wurde ein Sponsorbeitrag geleistet, um beim Turnier eine Galerie aufzubauen. Er, Heinz, habe dort dann seine Collagen, Skizzen und Möbelobjekte gezeigt, und die Leute seien sehr interessiert gewesen. 1996 veranstaltet er wiederum eine Aktion hoch oben in den Bergen. Jetzt wirft er seine Kuben vom Gipfel und überlässt die Gestaltung des Objektes dem Berg. Gerne höre ich Heinz zu, wenn er im leicht singenden Dialekt der heimischen Bevölkerung Geschichten erzählt. Und er erzählt mir auch von seinem nächsten Projekt, einem Hotel, als Plattform für die Kunst, die Hotelgäste werden in einer Galerie wohnen. Seine Augen leuchten.

VI *"Wie ein Menetekel erhebt sich heute ein Kran über jenem Gesamtkunstwerk.* INTO the hotel *ist geschlossen. Grund: eine Fehde unter Freunden. Schärer, heisst es im Ort, war stocksauer, weil die Presse ihm zu wenig Aufmerksamkeit schenkte und statt dessen Julen als charismatischen kreativen Kopf des Hauses feierte. Hinzu kam, dass* INTO the hotel *gewisse Anfangsmängel zeigte. Schärer hat Julen den Partnervertrag aufgekündigt. Er wirft ihm vor, nicht nach Schweizer SIA-Normen gearbeitet zu haben, was ihm allerdings schon vorher bekannt gewesen sein muss. Und was Schärer damals schätzte, lässt er nun entrümpeln. Dem Gebäude ist die Seele genommen.*

Heinz Julen stellt jetzt in Zürich aus. Ein schwarzer Raum mit Porträts von 30 Personen. Alle waren an dem Projekt INTO the hotel *beteiligt. Vor jedem der Rahmen schimmert eine Kerze. Julen hat das Projekt mit seinen Mitteln begraben, mit den Mitteln eines Künstlers. Für ihn ist es ‹der letzte Raum einer Vision›.»*[1]

---

1 Von Tomas Niederberghaus, http://www.zeit.de/2000/50/Reisen/200050_zermatt.html

A SKY-BLUE BALCONY –
THINKING ABOUT HEINZ JULEN'S WORK

CORNELIA PROVIDOLI

I   Three white washbasins are mounted on a metal stand in the middle of the village. If you walk along the main street, turning left about half-way between the station and the church, towards the Migros supermarket and the tennis courts beyond, an object suddenly comes into view on the left-hand curbside. Water comes gushing out of all the taps, filling the gleaming basins to the brim, until it overflows, running down the already rusty drains, to the ground – drop after drop. A small brass plaque bears the inscription of a name, *Heinz Julen*, of a year, *1993*, and of a word: *Überfluss*.[1]

II   I leave the village at about 11 am headed towards Findeln. The sun scorches the brown rooftops huddled around the church. Crickets are chirping excitedly in the quivering grass, birds twitter feebly in the shrubs. From afar comes the tinkling of bells on electric automobiles and horse-drawn carriages – I can tell them apart only by their different rhythms. Down below, the village sounds busy. I catch a glimpse of the red cog-wheel railway struggling up the steep, curvy track from Täsch and crawling into the station to disgorge another load of tourists that have come to visit the village, making the hotel owners of the mountain village happy. Tablecloths flash white in the midday sun, waiters stand to attention outside sunburnt window ledges, while pearly laughter bubbles out of dusty backyards and into the village high-street. It is a midsummer's day. Corinna would have been pleased and would have picked black strawberries.

III   Heinz Julen, born in Zermatt on February 29, 1964, as the second of four children, began to concern himself in earnest with the creation of art at the age of sixteen, making his first attempts at painting. Having attended the one-year introductory course at the *Ecole cantonale des Beaux-Arts* in Sion, Switzerland, he returned to the village of his birth where he began to create his own personal artistic vocabulary, pulling out virtually all stops in the canon: painting, sculpture, assemblages, furniture and object design, open-air events and happenings recorded photographically and on video. As if that were not enough, he designed exhibition galleries and was the artistic manager of a cultural center.

He feels a spiritual kinship with Renaissance artists, who conceived of architecture as the queen of the arts. His artistic vision aims at creating its own universe, a kind of *Gesamtkunstwerk* which he would design, and hopefully realize, down to the most minute detail. His creativity is embedded in a deep spirituality and a religious world-view inspired by and rooted in his Catholic faith. His work is concerned with the formal conditions of a given purpose; consequently, the forms he invents follow functions. The point of departure of his work is utility – "the urgent moment," as he calls it.

He tolerates systemic defects and might even deliberately encourage them, if they brought him one step closer to the essence, to the core; if they helped him to gain insight. He creates mobile, fragile worlds in which everything may always turn out differently than initially intended.

Building his mountain studio, *Bergatelier Findeln,* in 1980, and its remodelling in 1989, must be considered among his key architectural projects. Among them also rank the design, planning and construction of *Vernissage,* a cultural center which opened in 1992. This is a partly-subterranean three-storey building in the center of the village of Zermatt, featuring a bar, a cinema and a concert hall, as well as a contemporary art gallery called *Kunsträume Zermatt.* It is the first comprehensive expression of Julen's vision of a place where various spatial functions and uses overlap and may even be adapted to the visitors' changing needs, and do so smoothly and within seconds, owing to specially-designed technical or mechanical devices. In the cinema, after the show, the marvelous swaying chandeliers whir back to their emplacements in the center of the auditorium after having been pulled to the sides before the film begins – an homage to Jean Tinguely's kinetic scrap-metal sculptures. Julen himself designed all the furniture in the house, making a passionate statement about furniture and product design. From his very first artistic steps onwards, Julen has designed his own furniture – adaptable, mobile modules. In 1995 he realized the *Cube System,* which he presented in 1996 at Möbel Strebel AG in Aarau and at Kornschütte Luzern.[2] In 1993/1994, work began on the construction of *View House,* an apartment building for tourists. In 1997 Julen installed a mobile bar at the restaurant *Affenkasten* in Aarau, Switzerland. Also in 1997, in June, he started work on his most complex art and construction project to date, namely *INTO the hotel.* Officially inaugurated on February 29, 2000, it was closed only seven weeks later.

INTO was Julen's dream – this was his chance to perfect a the realization of his ideas, to promote his concept of a mobile, flexible combination of spaces and their use. Miraculous technical inventions turned his hotel into a magical *perpetuum mobile,* a chameleon-like structure that was capable of adapting and changing according to the needs of the moment. *INTO the hotel* also expressed a new conceptual element that may have lain dormant in his previous works, namely his interest in social processes and rules. Attempting to invert and remix existing patterns, he conveyed different values and created places and spaces for mental, spiritual, and sensorial stimulation. He did so in perfect harmony with, and often based on, his fluctuating architectural modules. The hotel's one hundred staff members were totally integrated into the process of completing the hotel, investing themselves, regardless of their official positions in the hierarchy. Work areas were leisure areas, and vice-versa. This is how Julen described his concept for the bar module: "*INTO the bar* was the place for fleeting encounters, for a change of scenery and pace; an interlude, a pastime. It was located on a metal disc five meters across and designed in such a way that it could shift between four different floor levels. It would follow the needs of the people and adapt spatially, according to the time of day: high up in the morning, when the sun flooded the terrace, and the entrance-hall was at its brightest; by the lounge one floor below at noon or, if required, by the poolside. Come evening, it would be on the level of the exhibition-hall and the dining-room. *INTO the bar* 'broke the barrier' between those who served and were served; this was achieved by abolishing personal space, the servants' workspace. The bar was to be the homebase, providing a family setting for all the people working and living there."

IV In Findeln, a little below Julen's mountain studio, his elder sister has had a restaurant for some time. This is where Heinz grew up with his three sisters, and where he spent most of his childhood. On one's way through the house, the visitor discovers walls covered in family photographs, in black-and-white and color; all jammed close together and showing four young children with their parents. Happiness, love, warmth and harmony in all kinds of situations, captured on celluloid. Here and there, lovingly arranged bouquets on small wooden tables; chairs on stone slabs, a wooden cross. Wherever the eye roams, pristine nature and the impressive mountain, the Matterhorn. The house breathes history and vivid memories. This is the core.

V Martin and Julie are already there as I reach the Alp. It is a little after one. They are sitting outside on the wooden sundeck, sipping a glass of cool white wine. It is Monday, and there are tell-tale traces of a weekend spent with friends who seem to have left before lunch. Martin and Julie are the only ones still here. I'm happy to see them. I already know Martin from Zurich, but Julie is a stranger. When I ask Heinz about his artistic and architectural beginnings, he smiles and tells us the story of his father, and how as a youngster he used to help him remodel ancient Valais chalets. Also, when he was just a little boy in Findeln, he used to construct his own huts made of blankets and fur, old bits of wood and poles, and he would invite his sisters for tea: "When I was little I would go high up in the mountains and build these huts. They got better and better, and suddenly they even survived the severe winter months. I was so proud, I would decorate them, breathing life into them, and creating an atmosphere, and I invited my sisters to stay overnight. I was a child borne aloft by my creations, and my sisters liked it. And so I kept on, going further and further in my own world, a world of constructions, of experimenting and of potentialities. I never stopped, I never broke away from this route. I never wanted to do it differently. No, I built myself into my very own idiom, and more and more people wanted to read it and live in it."

Heinz is sitting in the "Eagle's Nest", drawing. He plans to use these drawings for his construction work; he is measuring and calculating. In my mind's eye, I can see his large desk cluttered with untold drawings and sheets of paper, the steep steps up to his place of invention and experimentation. A laboratory and an "experimentarium". Instead of walls, big glass windows surround the cockpit of creation, which reaches up to the sky through the open roof, almost seamlessly connecting the thinker with the universe.

Martin and Julie leave to take the train down to the village. Heinz tells me about his dream of the total integration of art into everyday life. He considers it a challenge to always find new experimental platforms for art. He had his first exhibition as a teenager, in the basement of a clothing boutique in Zermatt, immediately proceeding to convert that basement into an art gallery. A few years later, he lugged the sculptures and objects created in his mountain studio to several mountain peaks in his vicinity. It was an event that he documented with photos and videos. In 1990, he was able to present his works during the international women's tennis tournament in Zürich. The Swiss publishing house, *Tages-Anzeiger-Gruppe,* sponsored an art gallery at the tournament, where he presented his collages, sketches and furniture objects, arousing great interest. In 1996 he again staged an event high up in the mountains, this time tossing cubes down from the peak, letting the mountain shape the objects.

I enjoy listening to Heinz telling his stories in the slightly sing-song dialect of his people. He also tells me about his next project, a hotel as a platform of art; the guests will be staying at an art gallery. His eyes are bright.

VI *"Like a bad omen a crane rises above the* Gesamtkunstwerk. INTO the hotel *is closed. The reason: a quarrel among friends. Schärer,*[3] *it is said in the village, was angry because the media didn't pay him enough attention, celebrating Julen as the charismatic, creative head of the house instead. Also,* INTO the hotel *had teething problems. Schärer terminated his partnership with Julen, reproaching him for having disregarded SIA norms.*[4] *Schärer must have known about this for some time, and what he liked then is now being demolished. The building has been robbed of its soul.*

Heinz Julen currently has a show in Zürich. It is a black room containing the portraits of 30 individuals who were all involved in the project, INTO the hotel. *A candle is burning in front of each one of the canvases. Julen has buried the project by his own means, those of an artist. To him this is ‹A vision's last room›."*[5]

---

1 Translator's note: The German word "Überfluss" has various meanings, among them "excess" and "overflow."
2 Translator's note: "Möbel Strebel AG" is a furniture shop, "Kornschütte" is a cultural centre in Lucerne, Switzerland.
3 Translator's note: Schärer is Alexander Schärer of the renowned Swiss furniture maker, UMS Haller.
4 Translator's note: SIA = Swiss Association of Engineers and Architects.
5 Tomas Niederberghaus in DIE ZEIT 2000/50, http://www.zeit.de/2000/50/Reisen/200050_zermatt.html

HEINZ JULEN – INDEX OF WORKS AND BIOGRAPHICAL DATA

29.02.1964	Born in Zermatt; grew up with his parents and 3 sisters, for the most part in the Findeln Alp area, above Zermatt, 2100m above sea level.
	Rebuilt various old houses in the Wallis canton with his father
1980	Started building his first mountain workshop in Findeln
	First attempts at painting and compositions using objects
1982–83	Attended preparatory classes at the School of Beaux Arts in Sion
1984	Opening of the *Galerie Heinz Julen* built by him in the basement of a clothes shop in the heart of Zermatt. Only works by Heinz Julen were exhibited: furniture, paintings, sculptures
1986	Exhibition of sculptures on various mountain peaks around Zermatt for Film/Photos
1987	First workshop in Zermatt was built.
1988	Exhibition at the Rieder Gallery, Munich (objects and paintings)
1989	Enlargement of the mountain workshop in Findeln
	Three-month stay in New York
1990	Conversion of the Rudenhaus in Zermatt
	Expansion of the mountain workshop in Findeln
	Exhibition in Zurich: In the framework of the international Women's Tennis Tournament, sponsoring was obtained from the *Tages-Anzeiger* group for a gallery to be built there and in which Heinz Julen exhibited (furniture objects, drawings, sculptures, collages).
1991	First exhibition at the Andy Jllien Gallery, Zurich (religious objects and sculptures, drawings, photos)
1992	Opening of the *Vernissage* cultural center in Zermatt, planned and built by Heinz Julen.
	Opening exhibition: *Respekt* (Respect) (Work by Heinz Julen – with a catalogue)
1992–96	Director of the *Vernissage* cultural center. Organisation of various international concerts and exhibitions
1993	Religious work with Jesus- and Maria-representations
	One-month stay in Israel
	Exhibition at the Vernissage, Zermatt: seven private houses
	Exhibition at the Ludger Vlatten Gallery, Heidelberg

	Building of a workshop in the industrial zone in Zermatt from the remainders of the Zermatt art deco train station
	Exhibition at the Andy Jllien Gallery, Zurich: *Frigorsessel*
	Fountain sculpture *Überfluss* (Overflow); gift to the population of Zermatt
1993/94	Building of the *View House* in Zermatt
1994	Development of the *Cube Systems* (object/commodities/household utensils)
	Exhibition at the Wälchli Gallery: *Bergwürfel* (Mountain Cube) objects
	Exhibition at the Schönegg Gallery, Basel (objects, paintings)
1996	One-man-show at Kunst 96 in Zurich (Andy Jllien Gallery): *Bergwürfel* (Mountain Cube)
	Presentation of *Cube Systems* at Möbel Strebel AG in Aarau and in the Kornschütte Lucerne
	Building of a mobile Bar in Aarau *Affenkasten*
1997	First plans for *INTO the hotel* and opening up of the hotel grounds by means of a tunnel
	Opening of the *Enzo-Vrony* restaurant in Zermatt (conversion of a 200-year old Wallis house)
1998	Building of the *INTO the hotel* started
1999	Opening of the *Cœur des Alpes* hotel in Zermatt (concept, planning and partial completion)
2000 29/02:	Opening of the *INTO the hotel* in Zermatt
	Exhibition at Kunst 2000, Zurich: *Der letzte Raum einer Vision* (The Last Room of a Vision)
	Exhibition at the Vernissage, Zermatt: *Der letzte Raum einer Vision* (The Last Room of a Vision)
2001	Completion of the *INTO* employee houses and of a loft in Zermatt
2002	Exhibition at the Malmö Art Museum: *The Last Room of a Vision*

ADDITIONAL INFORMATION

Information on the artist Heinz Julen
www.heinzjulen.ch
www.kunstraeume.ch

The *Into the Object* object catalogue will be published in October 2002, ISBN 3-9522531-1-1, for more information: www.ajourneyinto.com

Dieses Buch wurde realisiert dank der freundlichen Unterstützung von:
This book was made possible thanks to the generous help of:

MAX COTTING, Zermatt

PETER FANCONI, Zürich

SMOKE FREY, Aarau

JOB HEILIJGERS, Armfoord

DR. CLAUS HIPP, Pfaffenhofen

FRITZ MEYER, Féchy

ANNI-FRID PRINCESS REUSS, Zermatt

JOHANNES RIETSCHEL, Zürich

WOLFGANG WEISENBACH, Bäriswil

sowie weiteren anonymen Mäzeninnen und Mäzenen
and the other supporters who prefer to remain anonymous

SPECIAL THANKS

With the greatest love and thanks to my parents, who always support me and suffered so much. To my dear sisters, Vrony, Leni and Moni, who carried the pain with me, and to their husbands, especially to Max Cotting. Thanks to Alex Schärer, who helped with and believed in our project with all his heart and all his love… and especially to those people who still believe in our *INTO* project, even though it has been knocked down… Thanks to my always-beloved friend Anni-Frid Princess Reuss; to Gustaf Peyron, to Göran Christenson, Claus Hipp, Fritz Meyer, Johannes Rietschel, Peter Fanconi, Wolfgang Weisenbach, Smoke Frey and Job Heilijgers. To Adi Mader and his charming daughter Noemi, Cornelia Strasser, Hanna Koller, Michel Clivaz, Christoph Parade, Cornelia Providoli and Margret Powell-Joss. To Margrit Strasser and Frank E. Strasser for a lot of reading. To Heiner Orth, Christian Davi, Christof Neracher, Michael Hertig, Adrian Weyermann, who helped us to produce this book. Thanks to my right hand Julius Andenmatten; to Augustino and Paulo; to José; to Martin and Gerda Schnidrig, who got married as result of the project! To Martina Graf for all her love and her personal support; to Sasha Huber; to Denise Moll; to Chantal Michel, Gabriela Clemont, Max Wettach; to Silvia Gertsch and Xerxes Ach; to Patricia Fässler; to Urs Biner; to Jobst Wagner; to Daniela Fanconi; to Roman Schöni. To Lothar Berchthold, Carlo Bommes, Mark Kronig, Martin Schorno and the *Vernissage* team; to Hans Rohr. To my friends André Girguis and Helmuth Kühn, Thomas Julen, Beat Schmid and Fernando Willisch. To Polmarc Petrig; to Simon Lutz. To Christoph and Anja Petrig. To my dear friends and moral supporters Robbie Williams and Pompi. To Pia Maurer – thanks for the praying. To our spiritual friend Josi Biner; to Jris and Vincent. To my ex-exhibitor Daniel Neuhaus; to Markus Odermatt and the whole *INTO the hotel* staff. To Jürgen Amann. And a very special thanks and love to all the people who worked on the project or helped to make it happen… The whole Schärer family, Roberto Medici, Urs Hug, Christian Rötlisberger and Balthasar Burkhard. Thanks to Charly Bayard, Peter Wenger and his people; Peter Meyer and his team; to Urs Gottier; to Erwin Sarni, Pelé, Amadée and Leander Imboden, their father and the whole team; to Donat and Diego Perren; to Fiori; to Martin (Gitz) and the whole team; to Willi Taugwalder and his team; to Rolf Gruber and his people; to the Sarbach brothers; to Adolf and Benedikt Schaller and their team; to André Arnold, Roli Imboden and their team; to Fredi Wütrich, Thomas Gasser, Zenger and the whole team, to Sebastian; to Lüti; to Philipp Kronig; to Pommer and his people. To all those who were involved in the project; to the "Gemeindeverwaltung Zermatt", Robert Guntern, Stephan Anthamatten, as well, the rest of the board… To the neighbours and the people of Zermatt who had to support a lot of noise and dust during the 3 years of my building period… sorry for that, and again, a great "thank you all" for being part of such a story… Last, but not least, I want to thank God, who kept his blessing hand over the project during the long and dangerous construction period…

BILDVERZEICHNIS / IMAGES

Alle Bilder von Heinz Julen, mit Ausnahme von: / All images by Heinz Julen except:

THOMAS ANDENMATTEN 120–127
GABRIELA CLEMONT 15 oben / top, 66 unten links / bottom left
SASHA HUBER 11
AUGUST JULEN 139
MARC KRONIG 15 unten / bottom, 72, 84–85
XAVIER LECOULTRE 53, 59, 73, 77
PIA MAURER 2–3
CHANTAL MICHEL 45, 66 unten rechts / bottom right
HEINER ORTH 39, 40, 41, 50, 58, 60, 65, 74 unten / bottom, 86
MAX WETTACH 30 oben links / top left, 32 unten / bottom, 33 unten rechts / bottom right

AUTOREN

MICHEL CLIVAZ

ARCH. DIPL. EPFT, VORSITZENDER DES VEREINS ZUR ERHALTUNG ALPINEN KUTURGUTS,
MITGLIED DES ZENTRALKOMITEES DES SCHWEIZER «HEIMATSCHUTZES»

ARCHITECT ETHZ (SWISS FEDERAL INSTITUTE OF TECHNOLOGY IN ZÜRICH);
CHAIRMAN OF THE ALPINE HERITAGE CLUB;
MEMBER OF THE CENTRAL COMMITTEE OF THE SWISS HERITAGE SOCIETY

CHRISTOPH PARADE

PROF. DIPL. ING., ARCHITEKT BDA, DÜSSELDORF
PROF. DIPL. ING., ARCHITECT BDA, DÜSSELDORF, GERMANY

CORNELIA PROVIDOLI

KUNSTHISTORIKERIN, LIC. PHIL. I
ART HISTORIAN, LIC. PHIL. I

CORNELIA STRASSER

STUDIUM DER ETHNOLOGIE, DEUTSCHEN LITERATUR UND PHILOSOPHIE, LIC. PHIL. I
STUDIES IN ETHNOLOGY, GERMAN LITERATURE AND PHILOSOPHY, LIC. PHIL. I

INTO THE PERFORMANCE (THE BOOK)

Konzept / Concept	Cornelia Strasser
	Adi Mader
Redaktion / Editor	Cornelia Strasser
Übersetzungen / Translations	Margret Powell-Joss
Gestaltung / Design	Hanna Koller
Fotografien / Photographs	Heinz Julen, Heiner Orth, Marc Kronig, Sasha Huber, Chantal Michel, Gabriela Clemont, Thomas Andenmatten
Produktion / Producer	Adi Mader
Druck / Printing	Druckerei Odermatt, Dallenwil
Bindung / Binding	Schumacher AG, Schmitten
Herausgeber / Publisher	Kunstmuseum Malmö
Verlag / Publishing	a journey into … publishing
	Tel. +41 043 311 05 11
	mail@ajourneyinto.com

Die Deutsche Bibliothek – CIP-Einheitsaufnahme / (The German Library) – CIP record
Into the Performance: Heinz Julen and His Hotel in Zermatt,
mit Texten von / with texts by Göran Christenson, Michel Clivaz, Christoph Parade, Cornelia Strasser, und Cornelia Providoli,
a journey into… publishing, 2002
ISBN 3-9522531-0-3

INTO THE PERFORMANCE (THE MOVIE)

Konzept / Concept	Cornelia Strasser
	Adi Mader
Realisation / Director	Cornelia Strasser
Kamera / Cameras	Heinz Julen
	Christian Davi
	Chantal Michel
Ton / Sound	Christof Neracher
Musik / Music	Adrian Weyermann
Schnitt / Editing	Michael Hertig
Produktion / Producers	Hugo Film, Zürich
	Adi Mader
Verlag / Publishing	a journey into … publishing

© Texte und Bilder bei / Text and images by Ars Marobaa
© 2002 dieser Ausgabe bei / of this edition by a journey into … publishing

Dieses Werk ist urheberrechtlich geschützt. Sämtliche Arten der Vervielfältigung oder der Wiedergabe dieses Werkes oder von Teilen hiervon – wie insbesondere der Nachdruck von Text oder Bildern, der Vortrag, die Aufführung und die Vorführung – sind nur im Rahmen der gesetzlichen Bestimmungen zulässig. Dies gilt auch für alle sonstigen Arten der Nutzung, wie z.B. die Übersetzung, die Entnahme von Schaubildern, die Verfilmung und die Sendung. Zuwiderhandlungen werden verfolgt.

This work is copyrighted. All rights reserved. No part of this publication may be reproduced, stored in a retrieval system, or transmitted in any form or by any means, electronic, mechanical, photocopying, recording or otherwise, without the prior permission of the publishers. Violators will be prosecuted.